FAITH LEGACY

FAITH LEGACY

six values to shape your child's journey

Jim and Jerolyn Bogear

Compliments of...
wesleyan publishing house
P.O. Box 50434
Indianapolis, IN 46250-0434

Call: 800.493.7539 • Fax: 800.788.3535
E-mail: wph@wesleyan.org • Online: www.wesleyan.org/wph
Please send copies of any review or mention.

wesleyan
publishing
house
Indianapolis, Indiana

Copyright © 2009 by Jim & Jerolyn Bogear
Published by Wesleyan Publishing House
Indianapolis, Indiana 46250
Printed in the United States of America
ISBN: 978-0-89827-427-1

Library of Congress Cataloging-in-Publication Data

Bogear, Jim.
Faith legacy : six values to shape your child's journey / Jim and Jerolyn Bogear.
    p. cm.
Includes bibliographical references (p.).
ISBN 978-0-89827-427-1
1. Child rearing--Religious aspects--Christianity. 2. Parents--Religious life. 3. Values.
I. Bogear, Jerolyn. II. Title.
BV4529.B625 2009
248.8'45--dc22
                                        2009029046

Author Photo: Courtesy of *Captured by Joelle*

We dedicate this book to our three amazing children—
Lauren Delyn, Shaphan James, and Gabrielle Esther—who taught
us so many lessons about life, love, and laughter.

Live the legacy.

CONTENTS

ACKNOWLEDGMENTS

We must first thank our parents, Ron and Lois Bogear, Ron Brown Sr., and Mary Ruth Cox. We learned how to fully love our children because we were raised with such amazing, unconditional love. Our parents poured themselves into our lives, introducing us to our heavenly Father and molding us into the people we are today. We couldn't have asked for better examples to follow in raising our own three children. Your legacy lives on.

A huge thanks goes to Sally Tay Howe. She spent hours and hours of her rare, free time, revising this manuscript with us again and again. Without her help and direction, we would have not been ready to publish. (We now know the tedious practice of "mapping" a document.) Thanks for being such a dear friend and helping us reach our goal. You are truly amazing.

Thanks to all the Wesleyan Publishing House staff—especially Don Cady, Kevin Scott, Rachael Stevenson, Joe Jackson, and Dena Scott—for all the work and support to guide us "newbies" through this process. You all were great and made this a wonderful experience for us.

Finally, thank you to our family, friends, and our amazing church family for the support and encouragement you have given us through this process. You are dearly loved.

At the risk of sounding cliché, this book is truly a gift from the Lord. As messed up and imperfect as we humans are, it is only through His power that we are able to accomplish those things that last. Raising children is not an easy task. After all, they don't come with instruction books. But the Father so graciously guides us through His Word and His Spirit to pass on a legacy to our children that will better the generations to come. We give Him praise.

PREFACE

Next to the Lord, our kids are absolutely number one in our lives! We can't imagine three people we would rather spend time with than Lauren, Shay, and Gabby. They have brought us years of joy and learning, making us better parents and people for knowing them. We are truly blessed.

This book is for—and because of—our children. Parents carry a tremendous burden of responsibility to live a life that is worthy for our children to follow. They watch our every move. The decisions we make each day can affect them for the rest of their lives. With this in mind, we need to ask ourselves some key questions: Are we living a life our children can respect and want to emulate? Are we teaching them lasting values that will serve them well throughout their lives? Or are we just living in the moment from day to day and not doing that very well? Are we living for ourselves—our own things and self-promotion—or for something or

reater than ourselves, leaving a legacy for our children? When
e, what of our lives will live on in those who are closest to us—
our children?

Where the Legacy Begins

We've always tried to follow the Lord with all our hearts. That in
itself is a chore, since we all live in a world that is anti-Christ. Living
as "aliens and strangers" (1 Pet. 2:11) takes all our concentration and
effort each day. There's a reason Christ told us to take up our cross daily
(Luke 9:23) and follow Him. With so much focus and energy required
to live our own lives in Christ, how do we bring along with us young,
impressionable minds? What can we do to divide the time focused on
our own journey to include our children and direct their path?

Often our first thought about our children is for their physical care—
making enough money to clothe, house, feed, transport, and educate them.
But should that be our first thought? God gives us a higher calling and purpose—for ourselves and for our children. We're to "seek first his kingdom
and his righteousness, and all these things will be given to [us] as well"
(Matt. 6:33). If we are leading our children spiritually on the path the Lord
has directed, then God will take care of their physical needs. Of course,
we're not saying we should hole ourselves up in the mountains to sit
around, pray, and read the Scriptures all day—even though some days that
seems very appealing. We're directed to live in the world and to work hard.
But paying the bills should never be our primary focus or drive.

The Great Commission indicates that our purpose is to make and
mature disciples. This includes discipling our children. We happen to
homeschool our children, but when people ask us about it, we tend to
think of it more as discipling our children. This is not to say you can
only disciple your children if you homeschool; we believe we're all
called to disciple our children, and it begins at birth.

If you've picked up this book to figure out a way to get hold of your rebellious teenager, you've chosen a tough path. This process we're teaching is most effective when started during children's early years. But don't despair; the task is not hopeless. Many parents mistakenly think that once their children are teenagers there's nothing more they can do. You can still make an impact. Laurence Steinberg, professor of psychology at Temple University explains: "studies clearly show that good parenting continues to help teenagers develop in healthy ways, stay out of trouble, and do well in school."[1] Remember, in Christ, there is always hope. You'll just have to work a little harder to reach the goal.

It Begins With You

We may want to say discipling begins with our babies, but that's not entirely correct. Discipling begins with our own personal walk with the Lord. A disciple-maker models the attitudes and behaviors he or she is trying to instill in others. Look at Jesus. He never asked of His disciples anything He was not already doing himself. If we're trying to teach our children to have quiet time with God—reading the Word, praying, engaging in private worship—are they seeing *us* have a consistent quiet time? If we want our kids to be respectful of others, are they seeing *us* being respectful? Or do they hear us gossiping or bad-mouthing our bosses or berating the little ones we say we love so much? Do they see us criticizing others and grumbling about our jobs? Your children may not be able to see the hidden places of your heart and thoughts, but they can certainly see your behavior and hear your words, and this is how they're being shaped and molded. What kind of legacy are you going to choose for your children? It begins with you.

The Legacy Trip Idea

For us, the concept of a Legacy Trip began with the account of Christ's trip to the temple at the age of twelve (Luke 2:41–52). When Jesus was of age to become an adult, His parents took Him on a trip—a rite of passage. A few years ago, we heard about a friend taking a trip with his fourteen-year-old son. It was a trip designed to have fun together, but also to discuss the values he and his wife had tried to instill in their son. We decided this would be a great idea to develop with our children—the idea of living purposefully. We had to decide what God was calling us to instill in our children so they could grow up to be healthy followers of Jesus Christ. We knew it wouldn't just happen at age fourteen; it had to be an ongoing process, beginning when they were very young. We didn't consciously flesh these things out in writing when our oldest was little, but in retrospect we were putting a name to the values we had been instilling in our children up to that point.

This rite of passage was a "handing of the baton." By sharing intentionally with our children the values we had been working so hard to instill in them, we invited them to begin taking responsibility for embracing those values on their own. In essence, it said to them, "You are maturing into a young adult, and we want you to begin to own these values—not simply accept them as something we have wanted for you. It's time for you to take ownership and responsibility to live these out as your very own—to begin as a young adult to develop the legacy by which your life will in turn influence and impact others."

The Basis of This Book

In 2003, Jim preached a series on the Legacy Trip at our church, The River Church in Sacramento, California. We had such a positive response from the congregation and so many requests for a written version that we decided to put it into a book.

We hope you've picked up this book when your children are still very young so you can get a bigger jump on the process than we did. If not, don't despair. You can still have an impact on your children's lives and values.

Maybe you won't choose to call the values the same names we did, and that's okay; the important thing is to base them on biblical principles. The process we used is certainly not the only way to disciple your children. All these ideas can be customized to your family as long as they're based in the Word of God. We just want to share our story with you, and we trust it'll be helpful to you in your journey with your children.

—Jim and Jerolyn Bogear

— *one* —

THE LEGACY TRIP

A mother takes her toddler for his first big-boy haircut. A father walks his daughter up to the door for the first day of kindergarten. The high school senior marches down the aisle in cap and gown. These are all rites of passage that mark important milestones in our lives. This is not a new concept; it has existed throughout time and across cultures. There are many rites of passage—from potty training to voting in your first presidential election. A Legacy Trip marks one of those passages.

WHAT IS A RITE OF PASSAGE?

Let's begin with the definition of a *rite*. A *rite* is "a prescribed form or manner governing the words or actions for a ceremony."[1] So a rite of passage involves moving ceremoniously from one stage of life to another.

Celebrations of rites of passage in the teenage years cut across all cultures. For example, many Native American cultures have a *vision quest* as a rite of passage. In traditional Lakota Indian culture, the seeker meets with the medicine man and then goes out to a solitary place, taking nothing with him. He remains in a ten-foot area for one to four days, waiting for a vision from Wakan Tanka.[2] Hispanic cultures have *quinceañera*, a candle-lighting ceremony for fifteen-year-old girls to signify coming into marriageable age.[3] In Japan, January 15 is a national holiday called *seijin no hi*. This traditional-garb ceremony signifies that those turning twenty years old during the calendar year have received the adult privileges of voting, drinking, and smoking.[4]

If you don't know where you are going,
you will wind up somewhere else.

—*Author Unknown*

Religious traditions have rites of passage as well. The Roman Catholics view confirmation as one of the seven sacraments and essential to a deepening communion with God. Protestant churches, however, view confirmation as a symbolic rite of conferring divine grace and a further step in the spiritual maturation of a teenager.[5]

In Judaism, the *bar mitzvah* has served as the rite of passage for thirteen-year-old boys since medieval times. More recently the *bat mitzvah* has been added to include twelve-year-old girls. Although this Jewish tradition is generally considered to be a ceremony of religious significance, it's actually a celebration of a child coming of age and assuming his or her full status and responsibility in the Jewish community.[6]

From the Bible, we know of Jesus' trip to the temple with His parents for the Feast of the Passover. The law commanded all adult males to attend three feasts—Passover, Pentecost, and Tabernacles. Jesus would have been attending with His father since the men usually took their families. Being twelve, Jesus would be preparing to take on His full responsibility as an adult the following year.

CREATING OUR OWN RITE OF PASSAGE

Following in the wake of long traditions of rites of passage, we have created a tradition for our children as they prepare to enter high school. Having served in student ministries for many years, we often saw that when children reach high school, they start pulling away from Mom and Dad and begin formulating their own opinions about life and their future. Physically, they're rarely present in the home due to sports, jobs, church activities, friends, and the freedom that comes with a driver's license. Although we have maintained a strong connection with our children in the high school years, we also wanted to try to capture the moment—before time flies and they are off to college—to reestablish in their minds a definite list of values we've tried to instill in them during the first fourteen years of their life.

As teenagers prepare to enter adulthood, there's a point when they must "take ownership" of the belief system we provide for them. They will begin to take on the responsibility of choosing, maintaining, and growing in their life values. For this reason, we believe it's important to provide a comprehensive review of what we've taught them up to this point. That's why we've chosen the Legacy Trip to occur at age fourteen, when our children are entering high school. This is when they begin their transformation into adults.

The Importance of Instilling Values

This transformation is a lengthy process, and the teenage years are a very critical time in our children's development. Besides the important social changes we've just discussed, there are biological factors that make this a challenging time as well. Recent scientific studies provide convincing evidence that parental involvement and guidance is a necessity during this crucial time. Dr. Jay Giedd of the National Institute of Mental Health has conducted extensive brain scan studies in analyzing the growth and maturation of the brain. Before his studies, scientists believed brain development was pretty much finished by the time a child was twelve. Giedd's studies, however, prove that a very important additional growth and "pruning" period in the brain occurs in the late teens, and that full development is not complete until the early twenties.

Even more interesting: The very last part of the brain to be fully developed is the portion that controls such functions as "planning, setting priorities, organizing thoughts, suppressing impulses, [and] weighing the consequences of one's actions."[7] In other words, during a time when an increase in hormone production ramps up the emotions, impulses, and physical development of our teens, the portion of the brain that controls risk taking, rational decision making, and evaluation of consequences is not yet ready to compensate for these changes. There are biological reasons, then, why adolescents have difficulty making mature decisions and comprehending the consequences of their choices.[8] The studies support what we have known for a very long time: Adolescents need a solid foundation of values and character to guide them through their transformation process. If they try to make this journey without a healthy moral and ethical foundation, the decisions they make could have lasting and devastating effects on their adult life. The Legacy Trip is an excellent time to reinforce key values during this growth period and prepare them for the road ahead.

The Challenge of Instilling Values

Parenting and instilling values in your child is not easy. It takes hard work and at times can be quite painful. Living in Sacramento, we enjoy many of the incredible places God created nearby. We like to take our kids to Lake Tahoe for skiing and snowboarding. It's absolutely beautiful. On one of our trips, near the end of the day, Gabby skied down the hill to us declaring that Shay got hurt. We were able to spot him quickly, just up the hill, so I (Jim) hiked up to him. Shay seemed okay from a distance so I wasn't too concerned. But by the time I got to Shay, he was complaining about his wrist. This is unusual because Shay has a pretty high pain tolerance. When we arrived at the medical station, they quickly diagnosed that his wrist was broken; we needed to head to a hospital or urgent care.

According to Jewish law, when Jewish children reach the age of majority (generally thirteen years for boys and twelve for girls) they become responsible for their actions, and "become a Bar or Bat Mitzvah." Prior to this, the child's parents are responsible for the child's adherence to Jewish law and tradition and, after this age, children bear their own responsibility for Jewish ritual law, tradition, and ethics and are privileged to participate in all areas of Jewish community life.

—wikipedia.org/wiki/Bar_mitzvahs

We loaded up the family and drove into the small town of Truckee. There, in a small house, was the Urgent Care. The doctor was terrific. He had worked on world-renowned skiers and definitely knew what he was doing. Then came the "fun" part. After an x-ray, the doctor said, "We're going to have to work hard to get this bone set properly. It was a nasty break, and if we don't set it properly, it might never heal correctly." Since Shay loves playing baseball, it was important to all of us that we get it right.

The doctor had Shay and me go into a different room, leaving our family, including his little sister, right outside in the "waiting room." Remember, this was a small house converted for urgent care. They were literally right there next to us. The doctor told me, "This is going to hurt. But to do it right, I need you to hold your son down while I attempt to set this bone correctly."

Wow, you have got to be kidding me. I know it hurt my son, but I'm convinced it was so much harder to hold him down. *Please just let me take this one for him and break my arm*, was the thought going through my brain. The doctor laid Shay on the table, grabbed his arm, braced the arm against his thigh and yanked the hand and wrist outward to try to get the bone lined back up to heal properly. The scream was so loud . . . and that was

LEGACY TRIP IDEA #1
Visit a national park
(www.nps.gov).

just me. Seriously, Shay screamed as I held him down and attempted to convince him that this was the best way to fix his arm and that he was all right. Gabby heard her big brother scream in the room right next to her and became very upset. My parents were with us, so Grandpa took Gabby outside. Now, here is part of the kicker: We had to go back to x-ray to see if the doctor had gotten it right. He didn't, and after four x-rays and three attempts just like the first one I described, with me almost lying on top of Shay holding him down each time, the doctor was finally convinced he had it right.

The broken bone healed and all was well, but this story illustrates how we can sometimes feel as we are working on building values into our children. We know that establishing, teaching, modeling, and "encouraging" these core values to be lived out in our children is tough work. In fact, it may be painful and even feel like we're hurting our kids by holding them down to set the value in place. It's work and it's painful, but just like God the Father allowed His Son to die for us, it was for the best. We must stay the course and see the big picture. Holding Shay down was the best thing for him, even though at the time it made no sense to him. The same is true with our core values. We must do what is best for our children. They may not like it or understand at the time why we would do such a thing, but the pain endured is best for the "healing of the bones" and helping our children to be all God desires.

A Celebration of the Child

In addition to being a time to confirm values, the Legacy Trip is also a special time for Dad, the spiritual and practical head of our home, to spend with our child. Our home is very traditional—Dad is the breadwinner and Mom is the homemaker and nurturer. On top of that, I (Jerolyn) homeschooled our three children, so I had an unusually large quantity of quality time with our kids. Although Jim is very involved in our children's lives, the Legacy Trip gives him a chance to spend concentrated time alone with the kids he typically doesn't get on a day-to-day basis. Your home may be different, and you may decide Mom will take the trip, or that both parents will go. Maybe an aunt, uncle, or grandparent takes your teenager. It really doesn't matter who takes them through the process. As long as you have at least one adult, one teenager, and a plan, you're good to go. The important thing is to do it.

CALLING ALL TRAVEL AGENTS

Begin with a purposeful plan. We chose a vacation away from home, but you may decide to stay local or not even leave home—just design certain days set aside for this event. We planned a trip—they chose the location; we set the agenda. We wanted fun and wonderful activities designed just for our child—a trip that would create the experience to make the memory. Make it special, however you choose to do it.

Our firstborn, Lauren, loves drama and music, so New York City was her destination. We set it up like any other vacation, keeping in mind the child and her interests. Of course, Broadway had to come into the picture, so we purchased tickets and made reservations.

Shay loves to golf, so Monterey was his destination for some of the best golfing in the world. Gabby's trip, just last summer, was to various roller coasters across the country—big and fast.

Obviously, we put a lot of time and money into the kids' trips, but we *are* the authors of the book, right? It was a bit of a sacrifice, but we felt that this was an investment into our children's lives that we could not pass over. If you're unable or choose not to go away, you can still make the experience significant in your child's life. Get out of the house and away from phones, TVs, iPods, and computers. Unplug from the world to plug in to your relationship. It'll be worth it.

Before You Go

Before leaving on our children's trips, we each wrote letters to them to be opened at appropriate times on the trip. The letters put in words just how tremendously proud we were and are of them and the young adults they were becoming. Another great idea, which we didn't think to do with Lauren but did with Shay, is to ask other people who are significant to your teenager to write letters, as well. These letters affirm your children and encourage them to believe in who they are. Parents are expected to think their kids are great, but when they hear it from someone else, it's sometimes that much more convincing. In these letters, your children will see themselves through another person's eyes—persons they respect and admire. With Shay, we asked a couple of men in the church to write to him as men to a soon-to-be man. They gave some advice in the letters, but mostly they affirmed and applauded Shay for the life he was living. As you can imagine, those letters are just as special to us as they are to Shay, as we hear other people loving our child.

Vacationing With Purpose

Once all the plans were made for Lauren's Legacy Trip, she and Jim were off to New York City. (For simplicity's sake and since she was our guinea pig, we will focus on Lauren's Legacy Trip as an example.) New York City sounds like a fun trip, huh? So where did the value discussions come in? Well, they didn't spend every day, all day sitting around talking about this value or that one. Lauren could only look at her dad for so long. But they did focus on one value per day. Throughout the day, Jim would bring up the value; or at other times, maybe during a meal, they had a more con-

LEGACY TRIP IDEA #2

Visit your child's favorite city or a city that has activities and events related to your child's interests.

centrated discussion. Lauren and Jim made a particular value their focus for the day. It's your job to keep your eyes open for opportunities to apply the value through life's activities and to set aside the time to sit and purposefully discuss the value. You know your children and how they best learn. Speak to their learning style and the discussion will stick with them much longer. In appendix C, we provide Trip Notes that list a set of questions for each core value; these can help get your discussions going. Appendix D offers a Travel Log. Using these journal pages, you can record your impressions of the day and impart personal wisdom to your children. Your children can review the core value and establish an action plan for their lives. Both the Trip Notes and the Travel Log will become an invaluable tool to you and your child on the trip and after you return home. The Legacy Trip doesn't end when the suitcases are unpacked. In fact, it's really only the beginning.

You're Not the Only Wise Guy

Invite other people to speak into your child's life. Not only can you take letters from others with you and open them throughout the week, but maybe you can have a meal with someone who can speak the truth to your child. We have very dear friends, Matt and Lori Krueger, who lived in Connecticut. After a few days in New York City, Lauren and I (Jim) took the train to Hartford to visit them as a purposeful part of the trip. The day we were there, the value discussed was purity. Matt and Lori talked to Lauren about the value of remaining pure before marriage and what that meant to them and their marriage. Here was an opportunity for Lauren to not just hear what may have been perceived as preaching from her father, but the chance for another young couple whom she loved and admired to agree with the principle. Especially on such a sensitive subject, Lori and Matt's input was very important and validated what her dad was telling her. Dad wasn't just trying to keep all boys and fun away from his daughter. The Kruegers reinforced the point that this is biblical and for her own welfare. They also proved it's possible to remain pure no matter what the world may say. What great cooperation by the family of God to instill values into our children.

Live Out a Value

We also included service in our trip. Matt and Lori attended a church plant that meets in a school. This means setting up and tearing down stages, chairs, tables, and equipment every Sunday. So we went along on Sunday morning and helped transform a school gym into a sanctuary. We had a great time and actually got to live out one of the values while on the trip—generosity.

If you pay attention to what is happening around you, you will be able to find opportunities every day to live out each particular value. Helping an elderly couple with their groceries (generosity); pointing out to the cashier that you weren't charged enough (integrity); seeking the Lord's guidance for your day (devotion). It's not difficult to daily walk in these values. It just takes a focus on purposeful living.

Other Options

Your destination choices may be very different from Lauren, Shay, and Gabby's trips. Again, we chose to make the financial sacrifice to make the trips happen. But if trips are not in the budget, take one day a week for six weeks and spend time with your child discussing a value. Play ball together or sit down with a guitar and sing. Many parents have found that their children will interact with them over the controls of a video game system. The important thing is to create a memory through an activity your child enjoys, along with purposeful focus on values that will shape his or her life. These days will take time and planning, but they'll yield a lifetime of worth for your child.

two

THE LEGACY OF CHARACTER

Historically, a legacy was something of value that was handed down from one period of time to another, from one generation of a culture to the next, or perhaps some object or heritage passed down through families. In raising our children, it's our desire to leave a much more significant legacy than material possessions or family traditions, even though those are certainly nice things to pass along. Our greatest desire is to pass along the legacy of *character*; specifically, the character of Christ.

Our modern culture seems to put very little emphasis on character. For example, we can look at the people elected into political office. They're not usually selected because of their character; they win because they promise the things we want to hear. And whom do our young people often idolize? Musicians, actors, and sports celebrities . . . and our young people rarely consider the character of these celebrities they adore; instead, they're applauding and envying their accomplishments and cultural status, not who they really are. Oftentimes celebrity character flaws, even though made public, are simply overlooked as being "their private life." While our children may still admire a celebrity's accomplishments, we can teach them to be discerning and look elsewhere to learn how to live a life of character.

As Horace Greeley, a New York newspaper editor in the 1800s, wisely observed: "Fame is a vapor, popularity an accident, riches take wing, and only character endures." Our character is the essence of who we are. As such, there is no greater legacy we can leave than that of character.

THE BEST MODEL OF CHARACTER

When it comes to character, there's no greater example than Jesus Christ. To believers, Scripture says "clothe yourselves with the Lord Jesus Christ" (Rom. 13:14). That means taking on His character. We, as parents, want our children to revere people who virtuously live what they say and say what they live. God-made-in-flesh showed us how to live virtuously while struggling in this earthly body. He faced the same trials and temptations we face in being a person of character. Oh, they sometimes come in different forms than they did in Jesus' day—TV, movies, the Internet—but they're still ways to pull us down to a level below "the best" God desires for us. If the Enemy can get hold of us in the area of our character, he has all of us.

Oliver Wendell Holmes said, "What lies behind us and what lies before us are tiny matters compared to what lies within us." The greatest battle we face is the one within. Yes, the pressures outside our bodies are the temptations, but we must fight the carnal nature within, the element that strives to compromise our character standards. In God's Word, we find very specific guidance in how to deal with this struggle: "Be imitators of God, therefore, as dearly loved children and live a life of love, just as Christ loved us and gave himself up for us as a fragrant offering and sacrifice to God" (Eph. 5:1–2).

Leadership is a potent combination of strategy and character.
But if you must be without one, be without the strategy.

—*General Norman Schwarzkopf*

If we read further in the same passage, we can break down several issues and discover important questions to ask ourselves about how we're developing our own character:

> But among you there must not be even a hint of sexual immorality, or of any kind of impurity, or of greed, because these are improper for God's holy people. Nor should there be obscenity, foolish talk or coarse joking, which are out of place, but rather thanksgiving. For of this you can be sure: No immoral, impure or greedy person—such a man is an idolater—has any inheritance in the kingdom of Christ and of God. (Eph. 5:3–5)

From this passage, we can draw several penetrating questions and observations:

- What are we filling our minds with from TV, movies, or the Internet?
- Are we focusing on pursuing "things" rather than pursuing God?

- Are we set apart from the world, rather than being of the world?
- How are we talking to others? Are we lifting people up or putting them down?
- Are we practicing gratitude or complaint?

It can't be any clearer: We can't have our feet both in heaven and in the world—it's either/or. As followers of Christ, we are called to be set apart in our character. God calls us to a higher standard, and if we choose to follow the way of the world and its desires and lusts, we will not receive our inheritance of heaven. That's heavy stuff and it thoroughly underscores the urgency and necessity for a Christlike character.

You can observe a lot just by watching.

—*Yogi Berra*

The Word continues: "Let no one deceive you with empty words" (Eph. 5:6). Those include the lies that the media and society are espousing and that we so easily give in to, promising we'll be happier, prettier, more popular, or more powerful. The Bible says "because of such things God's wrath comes on those who are disobedient" (v. 6). His wrath? Do we want to experience the anger of the almighty Creator of the universe? We can't even begin to imagine what that would be like. Kids think an angry parent is bad. This is the granddaddy of all angry parents and then some! It's eternal.

The passage closes with a very simple sentence that gives the solution to the whole issue: "Therefore do not be partners with them" (Eph. 5:7).

Simple and effective: Don't partner with that stuff. Sin may be fun for a time, but the consequences are forever. We must ask ourselves and our children—is it really worth it? We know life can be tough, and the difficulties are not always of our own doing. Pain is imposed on innocent people every day. Despite this, we can choose to not live in filth or be pulled down into its dregs. *We* make the decision. We choose to succumb to the temptations around us

LEGACY TRIP IDEA #3

Our son Shay loves to golf, so we headed to the *Mecca* of golf on the West Coast, Pebble Beach. We had some great conversations about life and our core values, while attempting to conquer some challenging golf holes.

for temporary satisfaction, or we choose to fight the battle within for an eternal reward. It begins with us, our own choices, and then we must do everything we can to help our children be successful in their battles too.

READY FOR BATTLE

Are we on our own in this battle? Absolutely not! We don't have to fight these battles alone.

Character is self-control mastered by truth. Galatians 5:23 tells us self-control is one of the nine fruits of the Spirit. It's not born of self-determination, bestowed upon us by parents or friends, or acquired by power or money. It's from the Holy Spirit, as He lives within us. Yes, we must choose to resist temptation, but the power to do so comes from living in the power of the Spirit of God. Stand in the truth, and the Truth will stand in you. If our focus is to live for Christ, who is absolute truth, then we'll receive our power from Him. Standing in the truth is a simple concept to grasp, but not as simple to live. Character is developed as a daily discipline. It's a victory, not a gift. There's a reason id, "If anyone would come after me, he must deny himself and his cross daily and follow me" (Luke 9:23).

How do we deny ourselves? First, set aside time to spend with our Lord. How many of us tackle 101 things to do in a day and then say, "I don't have time to spend with God." It's a matter of choice. He so desires to help us through the struggles of life, but we need to know who He is by learning about Him in His Word, so that we can know the way He would handle the situations we face. In studying His character, we can better mirror it and be shaped by it. But if we spend little or no time learning about Him and His character, we'll have no idea what it looks like. And if we focus only on the stuff of this world (which, by the way, is presently and temporarily under the control of the Enemy), then that is what will come to the forefront of our character.

Children, obey your parents in the Lord, for this is right. "Honor your father and mother"—which is the first commandment with a promise—"that it may go well with you and that you may enjoy long life on the earth." Fathers, do not exasperate your children; instead, bring them up in the training and instruction of the Lord.

—*Ephesians 6:1–4*

A great illustration of this principle comes from the Royal Canadian Mounted Police. One of their jobs is to locate counterfeit money. In all their training, they never look at one piece of counterfeit money—they look only at the real thing. They learn it inside and out, frontward and backward. That way, when they do see currency that doesn't line up with the real thing, they know it's false. This is the way we want to live! We don't need the world to teach us how to live. We don't even need the world to teach us how not to live. All we need is the Truth to show us how to live the truth. We want the Creator to teach us how to be the creation He meant for us to be.

Psalm 1 says, "Blessed is the man who does not walk in the counsel of the wicked or stand in the way of sinners or sit in the seat of mockers. But his delight is in the law of the LORD, and on his law he meditates day and night" (vv. 1–2). This daily discipline of being in the Word and allowing the Lord to work in our lives is not just to obtain head knowledge; heart change must happen too. The apostle Paul says to "be transformed by the renewing of your mind" (Rom. 12:2).

Second, practice "staying near the water." The one who's being transformed into the likeness of Christ by learning from Him and walking in His knowledge will be living like Psalm 1:3 describes: "He is like a tree planted by streams of water, which yields its fruit in season and whose leaf does not wither." Ever been driving along and seen fields and fields and more fields and then suddenly a group of trees? If they're growing naturally, they're probably standing alongside water. Nature knows where the source of life is—near water—where a tree gets its staying power. It can't live without water. Jesus Christ is our river of life. He's the one source who will empower us to thrive and be fruitful. When we stay close to Him, we're better able to fight the battles, make the right choices, and build our character.

Third, we must "share the wealth." Knowledge and personal transformation cannot remain in isolation. This is part of taking up our cross daily and following Him (Luke 9:23). We must take the Word of truth implanted within us during our time spent with the Lord and go share it with a dark world just like Jesus did. Does this mean we're calling for door-to-door evangelists? No, we're calling for people to live out the truth of Jesus Christ by walking as a person of character; a person who lives a life devoted to, committed to, and glorifying the Lord. We

n "Truth Walkers." It can be done in any career. We have to
oney to live, but we live to minister. Part of the daily discipline
is not seeing life as drudgery, but as an opportunity to glorify God in
all we say, do, and think. The seeds we sow by living a life that glorifies God will direct others to the Kingdom.

CHARACTER IS THE FOUNDATION

Living a daily discipline of growing our character to be like Christ
will prepare us for whatever comes our way. Some people think their
character will step up a notch when they really need it; they think they
don't need to worry about good character until crunch time. (And even
though some may not espouse this philosophy, it certainly comes out
in the way they live.) However, true character is revealed, not developed, in times of crisis.

Stephen is a great example of this principle. He was a man who lived
for Christ. He fought for Him against the religious leaders who were persecuting the early church. In the end, he was stoned to death. When he
was being stoned, Stephen could have renounced everything he had said
and probably would have been allowed to live. But his character ran
much deeper; when he was facing a crisis—even death—Stephen's character prevailed. The book of Acts recounts Stephen's last moments on
this earth: "While they were stoning him, Stephen prayed, 'Lord Jesus,
receive my spirit.' Then he fell on his knees and cried out, 'Lord, do not
hold this sin against them.' When he had said this, he fell asleep" (Acts
7:59–60). Stephen's character remained firm in crisis because it was built
on truth, not on his circumstance, and was matured over time.

A few years ago, Jerolyn's grandmother had a stroke and was in a
coma for three days. When she awoke, her memory was completely
gone except for her husband's name and Jesus' name. She remembered

nothing, including that she had three daughters and seven grandchildren. After her daughters spent several days reprogramming her mind every waking moment, she finally started to regain her memories. The very first memory to come back was Scripture. Isn't that awesome? The Word of God was so imprinted on her heart that it was the first thought to resurface. True character revealed in crisis.

Former president Ronald Reagan said,

LEGACY TRIP IDEA #4

Our oldest child, Lauren, loves drama and the theater, so we flew to New York City. What a great location for many lessons, as well as some incredible sights and wonderful plays.

> The character that takes command in moments of crucial choices has already been determined by a thousand other choices made earlier in seemingly unimportant moments. It has been determined by all the "little" choices of years past—by all those times when the voice of conscience was at war with the voice of temptation . . . whispering the lie that "it really doesn't matter." It has been determined by all the day-to-day decisions made when life seemed easy and crises seemed far away—the decisions that, piece by piece, bit by bit, developed habits of discipline or of laziness; habits of self-sacrifice or self-indulgence; habits of duty and honor and integrity—or dishonor and shame.[1]

JESUS, THE LEGACY OF LIFE

In raising our children, it's our desire to model Christlike character. But this can't be accomplished through sheer willpower. It must be through surrender to the transforming power of Jesus Christ and a passionate pursuit of Him. We daily walk in the discipline of becoming more like Him through surrender to His will and spending time in His Word. We give control to the truth, and He prepares our character to face whatever challenges we may encounter.

Are we saying that only believers in Jesus Christ have good character? Absolutely not. There are thousands of people who demonstrate good character every day—they are "good" people. But our true character will eventually be revealed because it's housed in the depths of our soul, where it's guarded by God or by the Enemy.

For example, take two bottles of water, one containing pure water and the other holding tainted water, and place several nuts and bolts in each of them. Over time, the nuts and bolts begin to corrode in the impure water, just like our character flaws will show up and corrode our life. People may not see them at first, but they will eventually permeate and corrupt our life so it becomes dirty and tainted; these impurities will reveal our true character.

You see, without Jesus Christ, our "goodness" is only manufactured in imperfection, and those flaws will eventually come to light. To become like Christ—the ultimate example of a perfect character—we must receive Him as our Lord and Savior. Then He can work in us to be transformed into His likeness, not before.

If you haven't trusted Christ, our prayer is that you will accept Him as your Savior right now. It's very simple. Just say out loud or silently in your heart, "Dear Jesus, I am a sinner. I believe you died on the cross for my sins. I need your forgiveness. Please be Lord of my life. Thank you for cleansing me and beginning your work in my life to make me more like you. Amen."

This is the legacy we want to leave to our children and why we take the time to bless them with a special vacation of their own—to remind them as they are becoming adults to continue to pursue Christ and His character in their lives. We have no possessions or positions of honor we can leave to our children when we're gone—only the truth that can mold their lives and character, to take them through whatever they may face and raise them above it.

THE SIX CORE VALUES

We all live by a set of values. Every decision we make is governed by what values we have chosen to control our lives. If our value is money, then the decisions we make today will be made with the idea of how to get more money or to keep the money we already have. If our value is helping others, we'll look for opportunities to help. Our job is to direct our children into making the right value choices they'll follow for the rest of their lives.

In the following chapters, we'll discuss the values we've chosen for our children. As we said earlier, you may not choose these exact values, or you may call them by another name. The important thing is that all these values are biblically based and serve to help us become more like Christ as we passionately pursue Him and strive to serve Him daily.

Don't measure yourself by what you have accomplished,
but by what you should have accomplished with your ability.

—*John Wooden*

Each value chapter will start with a description of the core value and its foundation in biblical principles, including a biblical person as an illustration. Next we'll discuss how to model this value with our own lives and how to teach this value to our children. We'll give you age-appropriate activities with each value. Finally, we'll explain the question and gift that we chose to signify this value on our Legacy Trips. We chose a question to go with each value that would make that particular value stick in our kids' minds and challenge them to abide by it. We also attach a gift to each value. This is something they can put in their room or carry with them—forever—that's a tangible reminder of the instilled value. Visual reminders can sometimes be the best way to keep us mindful of where we have been and where we are going. (A practical suggestion here: When you find a gift you like, go ahead and purchase one for each of your children and maybe even one for yourself so you have a set. Just store them away until the child's Legacy Trip because it may be difficult to find that exact item again a few years later.) You may choose different gifts than we did; customize the ideas to your family and style.

The main idea during the Legacy Trip is to focus on one value a day and have some way to remember them when you get home. You decide the best way for you and your children to do that. Jerolyn's favorite one is the question. All the questions are hanging on the wall in our kitchen. We have been known to use them when disciplining to remind our children of the core value their behavior is not living up to. It's quick, easy, and they know exactly what we're talking about and what they need to do to correct the behavior. These core values put everyone in your family on the same page and set your growing child, soon to be an adult, in a "win" situation. We truly want to send them off fully equipped to face the world and its responsibilities as whole and holy adults.

three

DEVOTION

Gift: Skeleton key
Question: Who holds your key?

Jason tossed his baseball glove on the bed and flopped down next to it—dirty practice clothes and all. Staring up at the ceiling, he thought about the past couple of weeks. Baseball had lost some of its excitement even though he'd been playing so well. He was even on his way to MVP and All Conference Honors for the second year in a row.

"What's changed?" he wondered. Even as he asked the question, his heart already knew the answer—baseball had taken over his life. About three weeks ago, Jason's youth pastor had challenged the students to search out what things they were putting in front of their relationship with God. Ever since, Jason had been nagged with the feeling that maybe he was placing baseball before God. As Jason lay there staring blankly at the divots in the ceiling, he had to admit to himself, "Baseball has become my god."

The first core value, devotion, is taken directly from Mark 12:30, where Jesus says, "Love the Lord your God with all your heart and with all your soul and with all your mind and with all your strength." We have placed this value first, because it's first in our lives—above all, under all, in and around all. Loving God with all our heart, soul, mind, and strength is to truly love Him with our whole being. Whatever else we may do in raising our children, we *must* teach them to love our heavenly Father in every part of their lives through passionate pursuit of a relationship with Him.

When Gabby was a toddler she would hear me opening the door when I came in from work. She would raise her hands and say, "Hold you, Daddy. Hold you." I usually had my hands full, but I would drop what was in my hands and hold her as a loving father. God is waiting to hold us as we offer our full devotion.

Why doesn't Jesus just say "love God"? Why does He spell out to love God with your heart, soul, mind, and strength? Consider how we flippantly use the word *love* these days. "I love this restaurant! Oh, I love that car! Don't you just love this dress?" We use the word *love* to express appreciation of *anything*. Jesus tells us there's a deeper level to which our love must go. He didn't stop at just saying "love God," because we could give it the shallow, cursory acknowledgment we give loving anything else. Instead, He uses four additional words to qualify the kind and depth of love—*heart*, *soul*, *mind*, and *strength*. By doing so, He clarifies that this is more than just an empty, meaningless phrase God wants us to say. Instead it's "I love you with everything I am and all I have."

UNDERSTANDING DEVOTION

Love is not used as a noun; it's a verb. Love, then, is an action—a conscious decision that results in a deliberate act of communication to God. The way we communicate love to our Father is not simply with lip service, but with leg service as well. It is not only about who we are, but also about what we do. We must put feet to our faith and live out the love we have for Him. In this way, we help others to understand our love for God—a love that involves our entire heart, soul, mind, and strength.

Let's break it down even more. What does it mean to love with each of those elements—heart, soul, mind, and strength?

Heart

The heart is the center of the emotions. Often when we talk about loving something or someone, we talk about our hearts being captured or giving our hearts away. The emotions of the heart can cause a welling up within us that says, "I love you so much that I can't wait to be with you!"

Think what it's like in the early stages of a marriage; just the anticipation of seeing your spouse is exciting, wonderful, thrilling. We hope your experience has been similar to ours: The longer we're married, the more we love each other and the deeper our love grows. When we're apart for a time, we just want to come back and be together. An intimate relationship is filled with all the emotion of love, which results in an urgency to be with one another.

There's a great story about a mom who was home from work with her little boy. She was wearing a pair of old jeans and a ratty, torn sweater rather than her usual business attire of suit and high heels. Sitting at the breakfast table, her little boy looked up and said, "Mommy, you are so beautiful."

other smiled and said, "Son, why do you think Mommy is so ___ I'm in a tattered sweater and jeans. I have no makeup on. I haven't done my hair. I'm not in my business suit."

The boy interrupted. "Mommy, when you're dressed like that, I know you're all mine, and you're not going anywhere." What a wonderful shift in perspective!

Our heavenly Father wants to see us at times come running to Him, saying, "I'm all yours, and I'm dressed ready to just spend some time with you." That is heartfelt love. In this Scripture passage, Jesus is saying we are to love God more than anything or anyone else. No one thing or person compares to, or even comes close to, our love for God.

Soul

When Jesus talks about loving God with all our soul, He means our entire life. *Entire*, in this case, doesn't mean a length of time; instead, it means loving with all aspects of your life. We are to devote all we are to Him and be willing to surrender our lives to Him and for Him. This is what it means to glorify God with everything.

For Christians in many times and places, loving God with all their souls has meant to suffer persecution and even to die for their love of God. We're rarely faced with this concept in North America. Unlike many of our brothers and sisters around the world, we have no fear of worshiping openly, owning a Bible, or expressing our faith in God. Yet, in a year's time, over three hundred thousand people around the world will die because of their faith. They're martyrs, because they're willing to stand for the cause of Christ. That's what it means to love God with all our soul. There can be a cost to this kind of love—persecution or even death. Whether or not we ever face these extremes, God calls us to love at this level of devotion—a complete surrender to Him.

Mind

The third way in which we are to love God is with our mind—our entire mind. This means the intellect, the will, the decision to obey His commands, His ways, His laws, and His teachings. This is a conscious decision to love God and make the tough decisions when it's tough. It's not just doing things *right*; it's doing the *right things*. There's a difference, and sometimes the distinction is a tough one. For our children's sake, we must purposefully decide to model this: making a conscious decision to obey God's commands. That means if it's wrong by God's commands, no matter what the world says, it's wrong.

The difference between a successful person and others is not a lack of strength, not a lack of knowledge, but rather in a lack of will.

—*Vince Lombardi*

When our kids are struggling with making a right choice, we often ask "What's between your ears?"

They answer, "My brain."

"Who gave you your brain?"

"God."

"What does He want you to do with it?"

"Use it."

God has given us common sense, intellect, and a free will to choose. He's equipped us to think through the process. What are we doing with that? Are we using it? Are we choosing to follow God's laws, precepts, and ways? Allow God to renew you and strengthen your mind with His ways. Romans 12:2 says, "Be transformed by the renewing of your mind."

Are we allowing Him to purify our thoughts, or have we made them off limits to God? Are we serious about loving God with our minds? What about our motives? These begin with the thought life. To love God with all our mind is to consciously allow Him to transform us by the renewing of our mind.

LEGACY TRIP IDEA #5
Visit amusement parks. Gabby, our youngest, wanted to ride roller coasters. What a fitting way to talk to your teenage child about life's ups and downs! And what an analogy about life during the teenage years.

Loving God with all of our mind is tough! It's like asking our kids to focus only on their dad, and whatever Dad says goes for them. Think how easily they might be distracted by their own choices and plans, rationalizing it by thinking, "Dad really doesn't know what's best for me anyway."

In 2 Corinthians 10:5, Paul says to "take captive every thought." Sounds like an impossible feat! With the technology, the busy life, and the hectic pace we endure today, so many thoughts pop in and out of our brains that we may think there is no way we could take them captive. Still, Paul tells us to capture those thoughts for God's glory; to love Him with our mind by allowing those thoughts to be turned toward Him and turned over to Him. We can do it by the power of the Holy Spirit.

Strength

Finally, we are to love God with all our strength. The Greek word translated *strength* means "the actions of your body." This means putting feet to our faith. We may want to love people, but they won't see it until we're serious about it—until our love is tangibly communicated and acted out. His Word says to work "as unto the Lord." Everything we do should be for His honor and glory.

Most of us struggle with wanting to please others. We need affirmation. It's nice to have encouragement and an occasional pat on the back, and we certainly should be encouraging our children like that. But our service is for God only. When we worship and serve, it's for Him, not for everybody else. We work for and serve the audience of One.

A friend of mine (Jim) was setting up signs for Sunday service and began grumbling to himself about doing this mundane, thankless job week after week. Then God reminded him, "You're not doing it for other people. You're not doing it for Pastor Jim. You're not doing it for the church. You're doing it for me." This gave my friend a whole new perspective and attitude, and a change of heart.

We should work and serve with a debt of love and gratitude—to give our body and actions for His work, His kingdom, His glory. Sometimes it may take awhile for our hearts to catch up to our actions. But we can start with acts of serving God and following Him. The feelings will follow later. That's not hypocritical; it's commitment. We don't always feel love. If it were all about how we feel, some of us wouldn't get up tomorrow morning to go to work. We don't stop loving somebody because we don't feel like loving them today. Put feet to your faith and commit to say to your heavenly Father, "I will, with my actions, demonstrate love for you." *grow this church*

The greatest love ever demonstrated was by our Savior, Jesus Christ. He didn't *feel* like hanging on the cross. He sacrificed himself because He was committed to loving us. In fact, He said, "Father, if there's any way that this cup can pass from me, I humanly really don't want to go through this" (author's paraphrase). But because He was God, He said, "Not my will, but yours be done" (Luke 22:42).

Surrender is such a huge word for us in our Christian life. Jesus says, "If anyone would come after me, he must deny himself and take up his cross daily and follow me" (Luke 9:23). Not an easy command to obey, but a necessary action to take. Jesus showed us with His life how to live and love completely.

THE DEVOTION OF PETER

You may think there's no way to live out this core value of devotion: *It's too tough, and I'm too imperfect.* But take a look at Peter, a man who finally followed Jesus' example. He started out as a loud-mouthed, obnoxious egotist, but God chose to work through him in a beautiful way.

First, Peter went from being scared of men to being sold out for Christ. He was initially worried about what other people thought. In fact, he was so scared of men that he denied his Savior. In one night, he went from trying to cut off somebody's ear in defense of Christ to denying he even knew the Savior. Peter was worried about what other people thought and was afraid for his life.

Then Peter made a drastic turnaround and went from terror to surrender. Jesus reinstated Peter and said, "Peter, do you love me?"

Peter, sheepish and gun shy, was probably thinking, *I just denied you, Jesus, and you want me to love you?* But Peter answered, "Yes, I love you."

Jesus said, "Then follow me."

It's a beautiful story. This is where the transformation of Peter really begins. He was a follower of Christ, but real transformation began when Jesus said, "Peter, it doesn't matter what you've done; I love you enough. I want you to *know* I love you, and I accept your love and forgive you" (John 21:15–19, author's paraphrase). Jesus showed Peter such amazing grace!

Of all the disciples, Peter was typically the first one to give a response when Jesus asked questions. Peter didn't care if he was right; he just wanted to give an answer. He was known for sticking his foot in his mouth more than any other disciple. But none of the other disciples, and neither you nor I, ever walked on water. Peter was the one who got out of the boat (Matt. 14:22–33). Peter took some chances and began the slow transformation from egotist to activist. Peter still thought he was in the know and had everything figured out. Sometimes he would answer Jesus before Jesus asked the question. Once he tried to change Jesus' mind and received a sharp rebuke: "No way! Get away from me, Satan!" (Matt. 4:10; 16:23; Mark 8:33, author's paraphrase).

But what eventually happened with Peter? In Acts 2:1–13, we read about the Pentecost when the Holy Spirit came upon the believers, including Peter, in an amazing demonstration of God's power. Tongues of fire came from above and settled above the disciples' heads. They began to speak in all kinds of different languages the people from various regions and dialects understood. God gave the disciples the gift of languages.

The will to win is meaningless without the will to prepare!
—*Joe Gibbs*

Then in Acts 2:14, it says, "Then Peter stood up with the Eleven, raised his voice and addressed the crowd: 'Fellow Jews and all of you who live in Jerusalem, let me explain this to you; Listen carefully to what I say.'" Then the Holy Spirit came upon Peter and he went on to deliver a powerful sermon. Scripture says the people were begging the disciples to tell them how they could be saved. Peter said, "Repent and be baptized" (v. 38). God turned Peter's life around. He became the activist, the

r. He became the one who was the mouthpiece of God, and God
ter's strengths and sometimes his weaknesses for His glory.

Peter had come a long way from obnoxious egotist to an activist for
Christ. But he had one more step to take. In Acts 4, Peter and John were
being punished because they were proclaiming the name of Jesus.

> Then Peter, filled with the Holy Spirit, said to them: "Rulers and
> elders of the people! If we are being called to account today for an
> act of kindness shown to a cripple and are asked how he was healed,
> then know this, you and all the people of Israel: It is by the name of
> Jesus Christ of Nazareth, whom you crucified but whom God raised
> from the dead, that this man stands before you healed." (vv. 8–10)

In verse 12, he said, "Salvation is found in no one else, for there is
no other name under heaven given to men by which we must be saved."

Love the Lord your God with all your heart and with all your
soul and with all your mind and with all your strength.

—Mark 12:30

The Pharisees, the religious leaders of the time, noted that even
though these were ordinary men, they had been with Jesus (Acts 4:13).
Peter in essence responded, "I owe a debt; I can't shut up any longer.
I have to tell the truth. I have to proclaim what God has done for me. I
am no longer going to deny Him, but I owe a debt of gratitude. I am
loved so much that I will show my love to others." Peter finally got it.
And when he got it, he never forgot it.

What Peter got was that it wasn't about Peter. What we need to understand is that it's not about us. It's about God and His glory. We're His creation, so if God has made us, it's about God—following Him, serving Him, loving Him, and bringing honor and glory to Him, not to us. We can lose sight of that and think it's about us, but it isn't.

There's a bumper sticker you may have seen that says, "God is my Copilot." Let's really think about this: When we say God is my copilot, we're saying that it's about us. We get this image in our head that we're flying the plane, and God comes in and says, "Excuse me. Could I just sit over here, next to you, and while you're flying the plane maybe every once in a while I can mess with the controls? I'm your copilot, so maybe you could let me fly the plane when there's no turbulence and nothing around?" You see, we have it all wrong. It's not about us; it's about God. God doesn't need a copilot. He can fly the plane all by himself. God is able to handle everything; He's in control. So, when we love God with all our heart, soul, mind, and strength, we surrender all control; we don't even get to sit in the cockpit. Peter understood that he no longer had control of his life, God did. We are to follow wherever He leads. God can take care of himself, all by himself; but He chooses to use us, bless us, and minister to us and through us. But He can only use those who are completely surrendered to Him.

MODELING DEVOTION FOR OUR CHILDREN

Many of the steps to modeling devotion for our children are internal and may not always be noticed by those around you. But the results will definitely be external. The very life we're living will have the greatest impact in demonstrating for our children how to live a life of love toward God.

Surrender Your Heart

First, we must turn our hearts toward God. This comes through spending time with Him and meditating on His Word. We can't get to know someone or develop a love for them without spending time with them and getting to know who they are. Here's where some holy disciplines come into play, notching out of our schedules daily time with God through devotions, prayer, and worship. We learn about who He is through the Bible and who we are through prayer. Worship, whether with music, painting, writing, or silence gives Him glory and sets our hearts toward Him. The morning is a great time to dedicate to devotions. It begins your day with the right perspective and focus. Making this time a priority sets the tone for not only your day, but for your life. This is placing Christ first in your heart and allowing Him to be the center of your world.

Surrender Your Soul

But even the greatest intentions of the heart can become empty without the surrender of the soul. Loving God with all our soul means that we surrender our will to Him. He's already become our Savior through the forgiveness of our sins, but by surrendering our entire soul to Him, we place Him as Lord in our life.

In the 1970s, Bill Bright wrote a little booklet called *The Four Spiritual Laws*. It was an excellent tool to share the gospel with others. In it was a diagram—a circle with a chair in the middle of it. The circle represented our life and the chair represented the throne of our life. Whoever or whatever sits on that throne is the one in control. Before we receive Christ, an *s* for *self* is on the throne. But after Christ, a cross is on the throne to demonstrate that He's in control of our life.

About fifteen years ago, I (Jerolyn) realized that though I had allowed Christ into my life (the cross was inside the circle), I hadn't yet allowed

Him to take His place on the throne. I had placed my mother there instead. Having grown up with my mother as my very best friend, I was still allowing her opinions to decide my life rather than surrendering to God's will. Once I allowed Christ to take the throne, my life changed dramatically. God's Word came alive for me in a way I had never known before. Truths flew off the pages of Scripture and straight into my heart. Even decisions came more easily, because they were guided by His directing.

LEGACY TRIP IDEA #6
Attend a major sporting event together.

My attitude was positive, spurred by a faith exploding from my soul. Hope abounded because God was in control of all things. People began asking me why I was always smiling. The act of surrendering my soul to God was transforming. I had become a soldier for Christ and there was no turning back. I now served one Master, and every other voice around me was mere babbling.

How do you go about surrendering your soul to His will? You state what you believe and never go back. No compromise. As a soldier dutifully follows the orders of his or her superior, so we follow the orders of our Master and Lord. And He is trustworthy. We see but a pinhole into the future; He sees the panorama of eternity. Rest in his love for you while doing His will. He will never fail you.

Surrender Your Mind

When we surrender our soul to God, loving with our mind becomes much easier. Doing the right thing, no matter what, becomes almost automatic. It would be counterproductive to do something contrary to God's laws and teachings. If I am allowing Him to be Lord of my life, then I choose to follow His ways that I've learned through studying his Word. See how these all build on one another? I love Him with my heart by spending time with Him; love Him with my soul through surrender to His will; and love Him with my mind through following the teachings I have learned.

Surrender Your Strength

Now, even though following God's laws is a very logical step in loving Him, it's often in direct opposition to the way the world directs us to act. The world says to look out for number one. Jesus says to put others first. The world says to protect yourself, even if you have to lie. The Word says to not lie. The world says to seek pleasures that satisfy your yearnings. Jesus says that we will endure hardships for His name. Taking a stand for Christ comes at a price, but it also brings the greatest reward.

And you, my son Solomon, acknowledge the God of your father,
and serve him with wholehearted devotion and with a willing mind,
for the LORD searches every heart and understands every motive
behind the thoughts. If you seek him, he will be found by you.

—*1 Chronicles 28:9*

In our carnal nature, our mind will automatically go to the desires that satisfy our needs. But God promised that He can renew our minds and transform them into His way of thinking. Though we will battle temptations, we no longer have to be caught in the trap of selfishness. If we ask and obey, God will change our thinking to be in line with His laws. Thinking with the perspective of the Creator is the perfect place to be.

But these changes can't occur within us without spilling over to others. If we're truly surrendered to His ways in our entire life, we must look outward to others. We translate our attitudes, thoughts, and will into action. Serving others around us actively combats the selfishness that is the core of sin within us; our selfless acts glorify God. But we must be purposeful in our actions; they don't happen automatically. Plan ways you can serve others in your home, neighborhood, church, community, and world. Is a family member too tired to do the grocery shopping? Do it for them. Does a neighbor need help mowing the lawn? Mow it. Rock babies at church or help raise funds for the community library. Take a mission trip to another country to serve the people there. When you reach out to serve others, you're not only showing them love, you're loving God as well. He is glorified through our dedicated service.

We must serve Him at all times, not just when we *feel* like it. Loving God is a lifestyle, not an hourly job. We can't punch out when it's inconvenient to serve Him. Everyone will occasionally need short periods of rest from formal service, such as a position of responsibility in the church, but we shouldn't stay away for long. Our joy lies in serving the King, and we can do that every day by serving the people around us.

TEACHING DEVOTION TO OUR CHILDREN

It can be a simple process to teach your children this value, because children tend to be extreme mimickers. If you're living a life of consistently loving God, your children will see how to do it from watching you. But we can also purposefully direct their efforts toward that end. Remember, our children are combating the same enemy that wants to ensnare them with selfish desires. We can help them set boundaries and establish habits that will turn them toward God's ways.

Teach Spiritual Disciplines

Encourage them to have a time alone with God and study His Word. You can disciple them, leading them toward a love relationship with God and the surrender of their will to His. Pray with your children. Mealtimes and bedtime prayers are good, but pray with them when they're struggling about a decision. Teach them how to seek God's direction for their lives. Pray with them before school and ask God to help them recognize opportunities of sharing His love with their classmates.

Establish Boundaries

As your children develop good habits that show God's love, help mold their will to His ways. Our kids are bombarded with many temptations every day, so we need to pray for them to have the strength to resist. We must also establish boundaries to protect them as we can. But when they yield to their temptations, we should consistently discipline them for their actions. If we're going to be Christ-followers, then we're committing not just our own lives to God, but also to raise our children in His ways. If they're stepping outside His guidelines, it's our responsibility as parents to bring them back into line. Consistency and firmness will be our greatest challenges in this area. But the earlier you begin, the easier it will be.

Serve Others Together

As you cultivate their heart, soul, and mind, help your children love God with all their strength by including them in serving others. Bring them alongside as you serve. When setting up for a community event, take your child along to help. When making a meal for a sick neighbor, enlist your child's help in the preparation and delivery. Whenever you serve others, include your child in the process. It's

PRACTICAL IDEAS FOR TEACHING DEVOTION

All Ages

- Let your child "catch" you praying and reading God's Word.
- Let your conversations be permeated with wholesome talk, so your children will see and know your love for God.
- Pray with your children.
- Sing and play worship songs with your children.

Ages 2–5

- Read from a children's Bible. Share with your children how important God is and how important they are to God.
- Encourage your child to have Time Alone With God (TAWG). For younger children, start with just a few minutes to sit by themselves alone with God.
- Show your children how to love others with God's love. Take them with you when you serve others and involve them in the service.

Ages 6–10

- Give your elementary-aged children a Bible and a lengthier TAWG time. Provide guidelines for their time, such as listening to and reading only material that honors God. At this age, they many want to draw or even play quietly. Even this can be time alone with God.
- Discuss what your child is learning from God's Word. Work together with your child on any take-home materials from your church.
- Make decisions a matter of prayer. Ask "Have you prayed about that?"
- Teach your child what it means to give to God because you love Him. Tithing is a great start.
- Have a regular time for family devotions and prayer.
- Teach your child to love the unchurched by spending time with them.

Ages 11–17

- Encourage your child to go more in depth in their TAWG time. Be sure you are modeling the importance of time alone with God in your own life.
- Teach your child the SOAP method of studying the Word—Scripture, Observation, Application, and Prayer.
- When family decisions are made, explain how your family's devotion to God factors in the decision.
- When your children face situations where they must take a stand for Christ, support them and stand with them.

the best form of mentoring available. Your kids will learn to love others through watching you love others. Together, all of you will be glorifying the Lord.

QUESTION AND GIFT

Our gift for the core value of devotion is a skeleton key. We often say to our children, "Loving God means loving Him with your entire life. When God has the key to your heart, He has everything." For Lauren's Legacy Trip, we found a beautiful key framed and nestled in velvet.

Our question is, "Who holds your key?" The key we gave to Lauren was intended to remind her that she gave the key to her heart to her heavenly Father, and He has control. He has access to and can open any door—heart, soul, mind, and strength. It's a visual reminder for her to say, "God, you are in control and I love you with everything that I am. It's all about you."

Lord, I am so thankful for the sacrifice You made so I can live a victorious life and have eternity with You. Now help me to live the life You have given me in complete surrender to Your will. Help me model full devotion and train my child in living a surrendered life—heart, soul, mind, and strength. Amen.

— *four* —

INTEGRITY

Gift: Mirror

Question: How's the mirror looking?

Throughout his administration, Abraham Lincoln was a president under fire, especially during the scarring years of the Civil War. Though he knew he would make errors while in office, he resolved never to compromise his integrity. So strong was his resolve that he once said, "I desire to conduct the affairs of this administration that if, at the end, when I come to lay down the reins of power, I have lost every other friend on earth, I shall at least have one friend left, and that friend shall be down inside of me."

UNDERSTANDING INTEGRITY

What is *integrity*? It's sad, but not surprising, that this question requires a whole section to answer. Maybe the question should be "Where has integrity gone?" There was a day when a handshake would be a binding agreement; when you didn't have to suspect everyone of lying to you; when "no" meant no and "yes" meant yes; when a job well done took whatever amount of time it took, even though it may not fit into a nine-to-five workday. Unfortunately, people with real integrity seem to be in the minority rather than the norm these days. Truth and dependability are set aside like a last-resort option when they should be the *only* option.

Jerolyn worked in the construction industry. When she would admit a mistake to a contractor or an architect, he acted as if he were shocked that she would own up to it. They expected her to try to pass the buck to someone else. But a person of integrity is honest in word and deed. It's who we are when nobody is looking. It involves honesty, commitment, responsibility, credibility, loyalty, and a good work ethic.

Honesty

Integrity means living a life of truth at all times. Perhaps you've met people who show one face to you and then turn around and are a completely different person toward someone else. Maybe one is a façade of lovingkindness, and the other is back-biting gossip. Maybe one is ready to help with anything you need, and the other breaks commitments. We're left asking, "Which is the true person?"

Ephesians 6:14 says that when putting on the armor of God, the belt of truth is buckled around our waist. When soldiers in Paul's time put on their armor, the belt was intended to hold everything together. All the other armor depended on the belt to keep everything in place. This is a great word picture for truth. We can have salvation, righteousness, gospel, peace, faith, and the Spirit, but truth and honesty hold all of that armor together.

Second Kings 12:15 offers a thought-provoking description of an honest group of people: "They did not require an accounting from those to whom they gave the money to pay the workers, because they acted with complete honesty." Can it be said about you and your family that you consistently act in complete honesty? How are you developing a legacy of truth-telling and honesty for your children?

The man of integrity walks securely, but he who takes crooked paths will be found out.

—*Proverbs 10:9*

Jacob was so confident of his own integrity that he invited his father-in-law, Laban, to test it: "And my honesty will testify for me in the future, whenever you check on the wages you have paid me. Any goat in my possession that is not speckled or spotted, or any lamb that is not dark-colored, will be considered stolen" (Gen. 30:33). Jacob proved to Laban that he was truthful and honest—a person of integrity who lived his life by his word. As parents, we should commit to do the same.

Commitment and Responsibility

Integrity not only involves honesty and truth-telling, but includes doing what we have committed to do. I (Jerolyn) recently asked our son to empty the dishwasher. He said he would do it before going to bed because he was in the middle of a game. But the next morning, the dishes were not put away; he had not followed through on his commitment. By not keeping his word, our son damaged his credibility and, in a small way, brought his integrity into question.

We've combined commitment and responsibility into one category because first we make the commitment and then we take responsibility to carry it out. This component of integrity means meeting responsibilities, even when they're inconvenient. I recently got my teeth cleaned one afternoon. When I asked the dentist how his morning had been, he said he had a couple of "no-shows." They never phoned to cancel—just didn't show up. Now why would someone set an appointment and not keep it—they forgot, overslept, didn't feel like going? Whatever the reason, they had a commitment and chose not to follow through—not even with the courtesy of a phone call. It's easy to allow our actions to be governed by our feelings, rather than by a commitment to follow through. When we're governed by our feelings, more responsibilities typically go *undone* than *do* get done.

Have the courage to say no. Have the courage to face the truth.
Do the right thing because it is right. These are the magic
keys to living your life with integrity.

—W. Clement Stone

Responsibility and commitment boil down to self-leadership—disciplining ourselves to carry out our responsibilities and our obligations even if we don't feel like it, doing the right thing regardless of the circumstances. Responsibility and commitment means doing the right thing even when it's not comfortable and even in difficult circumstances. Proverbs 16:3 says, "Commit to the LORD whatever you do, and your plans will succeed." The word *commit* involves surrendering your desires and following through to trust and obey Him.

In 1 Chronicles 9:26, we read about some men who understood the value of commitment: "But the four principal gatekeepers, who were

Levites, were entrusted with the responsibility for the rooms and treasuries in the house of God." They would spend the night stationed around the house of God, because they had to guard it. Then they had charge of the key for opening it each morning. It's not likely that they were ever heard to say, "Hmm, I'm kind of tired. I don't think I'm going to open the tabernacle today." The priests were quite aware that their actions or inactions had consequences for more than just themselves. The same is true of us as parents. Everything we do or don't do directly affects those around us. Call it the domino effect. If we don't follow through on our commitments, someone else is going to lose out or have to work harder to cover where we failed. Fortunately, the Levites demonstrated a commitment to responsibility.

Credibility

Credibility is having the quality of being trusted. Such trust is established by a consistent pattern of honesty, commitment, and responsibility. James 5:12 says, "Above all, my brothers, do not swear—by heaven or by earth or by anything else. Let your "Yes" be yes, and your "No," no, or you will be condemned." In other words, we shouldn't make empty promises or meaningless responses, but if we say yes, make it be yes; or if we say no, be done with it. Our word is our promise. Consistently following through on commitments builds that credibility.

During the rebuilding of the wall in Jerusalem, Nehemiah challenged the Jews working with him. He said,

I also shook out the folds of my robe and said, "In this way may God shake out of his house and possessions every man who does not keep this promise. So may such a man be shaken out and emptied!"At this the whole assembly said, "Amen," and praised the LORD. And the people did as they had promised. (Neh. 5:13)

The people built the wall; they carried out the task with credibility in spite of overwhelming challenges.

We must teach our children by living the life we want them to live, and demonstrating integrity in our daily choices.

Loyalty

King David and his mighty men are a great example of loyalty. Not only did David understand and demonstrate this characteristic of loyalty, but as a leader, David received loyalty from his men—he lived it and earned it. First Chronicles 11:10 says, "These were the chiefs of David's mighty men—they, together with all Israel, gave his kingship strong support to extend it over the whole land, as the LORD had promised." *The Message* says it this way: "These are the chiefs of David's Mighty Men, the ones who linked arms with him as he took up his kingship, with all Israel joining in, helping him become king in just the way God had spoken regarding Israel." Later in the chapter, it lists men by name and then later lists the number of warriors under them. An amazing group of men! They gave David full loyalty and support and would do anything for him. To say it more in today's vernacular, they really did "have his back"!

I (Jim) have been blessed to have men like these around me in my ministry. It's one reason I've had success in the starting and growing of our local church body. No matter what happens, I know they are there for me. They pray, support, encourage, challenge, admonish, stretch, and help me grow as a leader. Loyalty is huge! It's not enough for people to agree with someone. Rather, it's important that they remain committed and loyal to one another even in the middle of disagreement.

For several years, I was privileged to serve on church staffs and learned the value of this characteristic, which had been instilled in me by my parents. Often I had a choice—to be loyal or to take a cheap shot. If, in fact, I could not be loyal—even if I was convinced that I was right about the situation—it didn't matter. I would choose to leave before I was ever disloyal! I always believed that if I could not be loyal, it was not the senior pastor's responsibility to leave; it was mine.

I remain friends with the three men I served under. To this day, they all still share a mutual respect and appreciation for each other. Loyalty is one of the key threads of this coat of integrity—*be loyal*!

Work Ethic

There are several Proverbs on this subject, but look at 10:4–5, "Lazy hands make a man poor, but diligent hands bring wealth. He who gathers crops in summer is a wise son, but he who sleeps during harvest is a disgraceful son." We, as Christians, need to make sure we have a good work ethic before we ever try to proclaim the gospel of Jesus Christ to people. If we don't, then they might look at our example and want nothing to do with Christianity. Hebrews 6:11–12 says, "We want each of you to show this same diligence to the very end, in order to make your hope sure. We do not want you to become lazy, but to imitate those who through faith and patience inherit what has been promised." Ecclesiastes 9:10 says, "Whatever your hand finds to do, do it with all your might." Don't be lazy; have a good work ethic. Work hard with every ounce of your being. Develop good habits for yourself and teach them to your children.

LEGACY TRIP IDEA #7

Plan a trip to Washington, D.C., and explore the Smithsonian.

THE INTEGRITY OF DAVID

King David modeled integrity. Psalm 78:72 reads, "And David shepherded them with integrity of heart; with skillful hands he led them." Now how can an adulterer and murderer have this glowing end-of-life summary? How can we say *integrity* and *David* in the same sentence? Great leader? No question. Mighty warrior? Absolutely. Man's man and make-it-happen kind of guy? Right again! And he could play the harp. But integrity?

David possessed both skill and soul. He had great abilities, and, more importantly, his heart was after God's heart. Whatever ability and talent or lack thereof we may have, we want more than anything to run after God's heart. And we desire for integrity to run through the very veins of our children.

Integrity is telling myself the truth.
And honesty is telling the truth to other people.

—*Spencer Johnson*

Even though David made some destructive choices, he also demonstrated several characteristics of integrity in his life. He was humble, while still being confident. Even as a young boy he was ready to do battle for his king and his King. No one was going to make fun of his God, not even a giant. But he understood that it was his God who would bring the victory through him. He was confident in his God more than in his own ability.

David lived for and loved his God, but he was also trustworthy and loyal to his earthly king. Though he knew he would someday replace Saul as king, he was Saul's number one warrior for a time. He served the king without the ego trip of wanting to have the king's job. David had been handpicked to replace Saul, but he waited for God's timing and acted with incredible integrity. Saul never had to question David's loyalty even after Saul attempted to kill him. David had plenty of opportunities and what seemed to be a valid reason to take Saul out and step in himself as king. But his integrity, humility, and heart for God would not allow him to cheapen the ride. John Maxwell in his *Leadership Bible* says this about David in regard to the throne, "David's honorable actions reveal his integrity and commitment to the legitimate holder of the throne, King Saul, 'the Lord's anointed.' David refused to usurp his power . . . David's greatness and influence vastly increased as those around him recognized he had committed himself to higher principles."[1]

As David progressed through life, becoming a leader and king, he lost sight of his commitment and became caught up in his own success. He was eventually brought to a point of brokenness, which then led to humility. Once again, he caught a glimpse of his God and his own heart. After his affair with Bathsheba and murder of Uriah, Nathan confronted him (2 Sam. 12). What was he to do? Here is where we believe his integrity kicked in. His broken and humble spirit brought honest repentance.

David was in no way perfect. The more we look at his life, the more we see how far from perfect he was. So it is with our children—and ourselves. Integrity isn't about perfection; it never was. Integrity is about our heart, our character, who we really are when no one is looking.

David didn't simply write a chapter on integrity; he lived it out, modeled it, and demonstrated it as a part of who he was and how he lived. David's mighty men were loyal to him, and he demonstrated loyalty to them. He could be trusted! Integrity is huge; it's why so many men were loyal to King David until death. In 2 Samuel 23:13–17, David expressed how nice it would be to have some fresh, cold, sweet-to-the-taste water. David didn't demand it or even request it; it was as if he was simply thinking out loud. What happened? Immediately, without thought for their own lives, some of his men went behind enemy lines and brought back water for David from a well near Bethlehem. When they returned, David was so blown away by their sacrifice, he couldn't even drink it. While other men were doing battle on David's behalf, he felt it wrong to indulge in such a selfish luxury. So, out of respect for his men and their sacrifice, he poured the water out on the ground. Now I (Jim) admit that when I first read this story, I thought, *If I had been one of the men who risked my life for that jug of water, and David poured it out, I would have been pretty angry.* But then I realized it showed what a big man David was. David's leadership integrity was heightened in the eyes of his men that day. They would do *anything* for him.

David was not perfect and neither are we. Interestingly, both skill and soul are mentioned in Psalm 78:72: "And David shepherded them with integrity of heart; with skillful hands he led them." Many people with incredible gifts and talent have crashed and burned never to be heard from again. They had skill without the soul. Just as David was chosen by God and blessed to be picked as king, our children have been created by God and are uniquely designed to fulfill His potential in them. To finish strong as people with integrity is one of the highest callings we can have as individuals. We hope, when our children finish the race, it can be said of them that they were shaped "after God's own heart."

MODELING INTEGRITY FOR OUR CHILDREN

Modeling a life of integrity is not an easy task in modern society. Many men and women who are public figures fall from tremendous heights when they're not able to live up to the challenge of integrity. They seem to believe they're autonomous and don't have to answer to anyone—a dangerous position to take. In doing so, they attempt to place themselves above some or all moral laws—the very laws that become their downfall. Ordinary people often do exactly the same thing. By looking out for number one at any cost, we arrogantly position ourselves to act in whatever way seems beneficial to us. *Truth-telling* is the way to break the pattern.

LEGACY TRIP IDEA #8
Take a trip to the country
of your ancestry.

The points we have discussed so far—honesty, commitment and responsibility, credibility, loyalty, and work ethic all have a foundation in truth-telling. We must make our word worth something by doing what we say we will do. If we don't, we're living in lies and our integrity is worthless.

Truth-Telling

To model integrity, we must first stop lying. Not only is this a command from God—"Do not lie" (Lev. 19:11)—but it's one of the sins that can completely destroy our credibility with others. Aristotle said, "Liars when they speak the truth are not believed." We've all bent a story to our advantage a time or two in a desire to make ourselves look better than we actually are. But we usually end up making ourselves look worse. In contrast, the Scripture says, "Speak the truth in love" (Eph. 4:15).

We should also be careful not to teach our children to lie *for* us: "I'm not here right now."

"Yes, you are."

"Well, just *tell* them I'm not here."

Not only does this model lying, but it also instructs our children in how to lie; by doing so, we condone the action.

As a young man, Stuart Briscoe, a pastor and author, began a new job in a bank. One day his boss said, "If Mr. So-and-so calls for me, tell him I'm out."

Briscoe replied, "Oh, are you planning to go somewhere?"

69

"No, I just do not want to speak to him, so tell him I am out," the boss replied.

"Let me make sure I understand," Briscoe said. "You want me to lie for you?"

That's when the boss blew. He couldn't believe his employee would challenge him. But God gave Stuart a flash of insight. He simply said, "Sir, you should be happy. Because if I won't lie *for* you, there's a pretty good chance I won't lie *to* you." Teach our kids to lie, and they may give it back to us.[2]

Follow Through

In maintaining integrity, when you ask others to make a commitment, make sure you're willing to make the same commitment. As leaders in our community, church, and jobs, we try to demonstrate and practice this principle daily. You're in a leadership position (if nothing else, as a parent), so model this value by not asking those under you to do something that you're not willing to do yourself.

And David shepherded them with integrity of heart;
with skillful hands he led them.

—*Psalm 78:72*

With credibility comes responsibility. My (Jim) dad taught me a long time ago that a handshake is as good as a contract. If you say you're going to do it, you are going to do it. If you make a promise and shake on it, unless something unavoidable happens that prevents you from getting there, you ought to carry through on your commitment. We shouldn't be the kind of person who only follows through if no better option comes along. We don't bail on a commitment simply because we've decided we don't want to get up and do it. We should be people of our word and ask no more of others than we require of ourselves.

Loyalty

Be a loyal friend. How many of us have had somebody who puts their arm around us, smiles, shakes our hand, and says nice things, then later on we hear what they said about us behind our backs? A person of integrity is one who is *loyal*. We've mentioned the armor of God described in Ephesians 6. Do you realize the armor covers every part of you except your back? Ever wonder why? First, you ought to be facing the enemy and going after them, but second, it is our responsibility to cover each other's backs. So when we're fighting the enemy, they can't come around us and stab us in the back because we have each other covered. We must be the kind of people who can truthfully say, "I'm looking out for you. I'm loyal and will not be the one who stabs you in the back when you are not looking."

Excellence

"Every day and in every way, do your best for God." This is a saying I (Jim) often bring up to our kids. Every day and in every way, do your best for God. That is a great work ethic. Go the extra mile. Work hard and go above what is asked of you. I worked for a package delivery company many years ago; it got me through college and graduate work. The bosses started watching how I worked—learning the job and the routes well, loading the trucks efficiently. One day they asked me to go into management. They told me that one of the things that impressed them most was how I went above and beyond what I was told to do. I told them, "Do you know why I do that? Your expectations to meet standards are pretty high, but the standard of excellence that my dad instilled in me and what I try to live is even higher. So when I reach your level, I still haven't reached the level that has been set for me already."

What standards are we setting for our children to reach? A few years ago, we asked one young lady to babysit for our kids. When we came home, she was on the phone. She didn't have any idea where our kids were or what they were doing. By the way, she only did that one time. On the other hand, we had another girl sit for us who lived a rather privileged lifestyle. We were a little concerned with how she was going to work out. She was, we thought, kind of spoiled. But we were pleasantly surprised by her work ethic. When we got home, the kids were bathed, the dishes put away, the dishwasher running, and the house was clean. She went above and beyond what she was asked to do. We paid her well! We wanted her to babysit every time. A person with good work ethic is highly valued. And a person of integrity has a good work ethic.

TEACHING OUR CHILDREN INTEGRITY

How do we teach all of these qualities of integrity to our kids?

Talk about Honesty

First, talk to your children about honesty. Teach them to always tell the truth—no white lies, no misleading, and no bending the truth. Living an integrity-filled life is not always easy. But we must teach our children to always tell the truth and help them to know they can't get away with just a half-truth. One of the things we try to practice in our home is truth-telling. I (Jerolyn) have often said to the children, "There's forgiveness, grace, and mercy, but don't lie to me or the consequences will be much worse!" Make the consequences of lying tough, so they learn the value of being a truth-teller.

Expect Responsibility

To raise a responsible person, develop disciplines of responsibility at an early age. Some of us are trying to be too gentle and loving by picking up after our kids when we need to teach them to pick up after themselves. At a young age, Gabby always fought us regarding dishwasher silverware duty. "I'm not big enough," she'd whine. "Sure you are; there's a stool. There's the drawer. Figure it out, learn it, and do it. There are more responsibilities where that came from; you're just getting started." It all begins when they're little. The rite of passage trip discussed in this book is to help our children as young adults to understand what we've been teaching them all their lives. True love trains them to be independent, responsible workers that carry their own weight. We need to teach our children to do for themselves.

We all need to have habits of daily discipline in our lives. Create a list of responsibilities and corresponding consequences and rewards for your children. If there are going to be consequences to their actions, good or bad, then we need to let them know what those consequences are up front, so everybody knows the ground rules.

These practices will help our children develop a good work ethic. Think about the kind of work ethic people had a couple of generations ago, along with an unwavering commitment. Parents taught responsibility at an early age and continued to help their children meet those responsibilities. We're doing our best to follow that same pattern. For example, in our home the children are not paid for doing chores. They are a part of the family, so they don't get recognition for helping maintain the home. Their reward is the privilege of being part of a family. Occasionally, jobs which go "above and beyond" may warrant an extra reward, but for the most part, we work together as a family—pitching in and helping to maintain the home we share together.

PRACTICAL IDEAS FOR TEACHING INTEGRITY

All Ages

- Establish consequences for lying.
- Expect your child to be a hard worker. No laziness allowed!
- Encourage your child to set the bar high on personal expectations.
- Insist that your child keep his or her word—"If you said you'd do it, do it."
- Have your child stick with responsibilities to a reasonable conclusion. For example, if you start on a ball team, complete the season. If you take piano lessons, finish the semester. If you sign up for a volunteer position, be there when you are scheduled or find a replacement.

Ages 2–5

- Teach the difference between a lie and the truth. Then enforce consequences for lying.
- Train your child to do small, manageable chores, like putting clean silverware away or picking up toys and putting them in a basket.
- Give them a responsibility that helps the family, like folding napkins for the dinner table.
- Praise your child when he or she helps out doing something that you didn't ask him or her to do.

Ages 6–10

- Establish a chore list. If you have more than one child, rotate the chores weekly for variety.
- Give your child a responsibility that helps others, like helping you volunteer at church or in the community.
- Talk to your child about loyalty to teachers, coaches, or other instructors. God has placed those people in authority.
- Set high expectations for your child's grades, while honoring the child's level of capability. Encouragement is huge at this age. Set boundaries on distractions like TV and the Internet.

Ages 11–17

- Involve your child in bigger responsibilities, like mowing the lawn, babysitting siblings, and running errands.
- Encourage your child to take on a volunteer responsibility of his or her own.
- Instruct your child to be loyal to a friend who hurts or betrays him or her. (It happens to every teenager at one time or another.)

continued

PRACTICAL IDEAS FOR TEACHING INTEGRITY

- Stay on top of what your child is doing in regards to homework and tests. Children are often tempted to slack off at this age. Inspire your child with ideas, encouragement, and praise. Continue to set boundaries on distractions like TV and the Internet.
- If your child has a job, ask his or her employer periodically about your child's work ethic. As a parent, you have every right to follow up.

Parents

- Be an example of always telling the truth. Your children are listening.
- Do not ask your child to lie for you.
- Keep your commitments.
- Always show loyalty to the authorities over you and to your spouse and kids. If you have complaints, don't do it in front of your kids.
- Be a volunteer at church and perhaps in other non-profit organizations.

Ensure Follow Through

After developing disciplines of responsibility, help your children make sure they carry out their commitments. What are we teaching our kids if we sign them up for an activity—drama, music, sports, or whatever—and then allow them to bail out in the middle? Now there are times when grades and other responsibilities are a higher priority, and we, as parents, have to pull the plug on an activity. Or there may be times when we have to discipline them by taking away one of their activities. What we're referring to, though, is when parents give in to the whiny plea: "I don't feel like it!" So we let them back out of the commitment because it's easier to let it go rather than fight a battle.

Instead, our response should be, "You have an obligation—an expectation to be a part of that team, that production, that whatever it is, and you're going to carry it out to completion. Now, at an appropriate stopping point, we can reevaluate your activities, but right now you need to finish your commitment."

Along those same lines, we need to do *our* part to help our kids keep their commitments. If they have made the commitment to an activity, we need to make sure they get there—not use the excuse of inconvenience to let them miss the event because we're too tired or put out. We need to be people of integrity, and consider how our own actions teach our children by example.

Instill Spiritual Discipline

Show your children disciplined habits. Teach them to pray at an early age; help them to spend time in God's Word to understand the power of prayer, and the life change it brings. Take them to worship on Sunday morning. Demonstrate the priority of corporate worship by consistently taking them yourself. The only option on Sunday morning ought to be church, not one of many options. Make it a priority. Make it a commitment.

Occasionally, your children may be asked to participate in activities that happen on Sunday morning. We're in that situation right now; our children were asked to play on special-invitation-type teams. The coaches know, however, our kids may only play in a certain number of games because they don't play on Sunday mornings. They know it up front. We've made that commitment clear. We had a situation a couple of years ago where we told the coach our son could play the weekend tournament, but he would not be playing on Sunday morning. The coach understood, and we really appreciated that. After the game on Saturday, the coach asked if somebody could pick up our son the next morning and take him to the game. I told him we had already made that decision—no. What are we teaching our children? Are we teaching them to love God with all their heart, soul, mind, and strength, or teaching them to "kind of" love God when it's convenient to our schedule? A person of integrity will remain disciplined in the "holy" habits God has established for us.

Encourage Loyalty

Teach your children to be loyal. We so appreciate our daughter, Lauren, in this. People have always said she is a loyal friend. Just recently, she risked a relationship because she needed to stand up to somebody on behalf of a friend. She was willing to take the risk of losing one relationship to defend another. This is definitely a challenge; it's difficult—but be loyal. We cannot say one thing to one person and another to somebody else. We all know how tempting it is to turn our back on someone when the situation becomes inconvenient or difficult. For students, it's easy to try to make everybody like them. But a person of integrity will not sacrifice a friend or relationship by being disloyal. Practice loyalty.

David says, "I will walk within my house in the integrity of my heart" (Ps. 101:2 NASB). When we are walking in our house—walking with those who watch us every day through every situation—are we people of integrity? Are we moms and dads, husbands and wives, men and women of integrity? What are we teaching our children through the life we are living? Author H. Jackson Brown Jr. said, "Live so that when your children think of fairness and integrity, they think of you."[3]

In order to set a clay pot in biblical times, the molded clay was put into a kiln and brought to a high heat. Sometimes the pots would come out with cracks in them. The potter might simply fill the cracks with hot wax and proceed to sell the pots. But when such a pot was heated, the wax would melt and whatever liquid was in the pot would leak out the cracks. Pots that came out of the kiln with no cracks were said to have integrity. The word *integrity* actually means wholeness or completeness.[4] So pots with no cracks or holes in them were pots of integrity. Live out your integrity in such a way that when the heat is on, there won't be any cracks found.

QUESTION AND GIFT

The gift for integrity is a mirror. The question we ask is, "Are you and God pleased with the person you see when you look in the mirror?" In other words, "How's the mirror looking?" Are you a person of integrity? Maybe we ought to add, "Are you and your family and God pleased?" Will our character end up representing a person of integrity—one who is honest, who keeps commitments, who has credibility, who is loyal, and who has a good work ethic? What kind of legacy are we pouring into the lives of our children? Are we being an example of a person with integrity? David says, "I will walk within my house in the integrity of my heart" (Ps. 101:2 NASB). How about you?

Lord, help me to walk within my house with integrity of heart. Holy Spirit, remind me to be a truth-teller, keep my commitments, and remain loyal. I pray my children will not only see these things in me, but with Your help that I will train them to the same end. May we be a family of integrity to a world that wants to see truth lived out. Amen.

— *five* —

PURITY

Gift: Ring
Question: What's on your hand?

Heather and Corrine sit on the front steps of their high school with their heads together as they talk excitedly. "Josh asked you to the prom? That's awesome!" exclaims Heather. "I heard he and the guys were renting a hotel room for after the dance. You know what that means."

"Heather, I don't know if I'm ready for that kind of step," Corrine says. "I've never done it."

"Oh, come on," says Heather. "You have to. Everybody else is. It's about time you start."

Josh and Brett hang around the locker room after practice discussing their plans for prom. "Did you get the suite reserved?" asks Josh.

"Yep," Brett replies. "This is going to be one hot after-prom party. You asked Heather to go, right?"

"Yeah, and I can't wait. We've been dating for two months now. It's about time."

UNDERSTANDING PURITY

Purity is not a hot topic in our society. Sensuality is. Could there be any greater force against the biblical value of purity? God created us as sensual beings. But the Enemy wants to distort the beautiful union that God designed to be enjoyed between one man and one woman. As parents, we need to model behavior that protects *our* purity and teach our children how to fight this battle that's so powerful and prevalent today.

When I (Jerolyn) was a teenager, I entered a speech contest. My topic was "Sex in Television." My main argument was the degeneration of sexual values portrayed in television over the years. I cited an *I Love Lucy* episode from the 1950s, when a TV husband and wife couldn't even be shown lying in the same bed. Instead of a queen or king bed, they had two twin beds set up with a nightstand in between. I compared those standards to what was being shown on TV in the 1970s. How much further down that road have we gone since my speech thirty years ago? Nothing is sacred anymore. And it's not just late-night adult shows. Programs targeted for teenagers are showing sex as a natural occurrence in the process of a growing relationship. We even have shows about unwed pregnant teenagers. Few movies, other than G-rated, are made without some sexual content. Music lyrics

Purity and simplicity are the two wings with which man
soars above the earth and all temporary nature.

—*Thomas à Kempis*

and videos are often totally centered on sensuality. Public displays of affection (PDA) in our schools is no longer forbidden or even considered taboo. TV commercials use sex to sell their products. Where will it go from here? How much more will be allowed before it stops?

We must do all we can to protect our children from the evils surrounding them. If they're standing at a cliff's edge with no handrail, we certainly will warn them to be careful and tell them to back away from the ledge. Shouldn't we offer the same protection for their purity? Our desire is for our children to remain sexually pure (abstinent) so they can present themselves completely to their spouse. Not an easy task with so many temptations around them. So how do we help them and ourselves to remain sexually pure?

THE PURITY OF JOSEPH

Even though Joseph was sold into slavery, his integrity and hard work earned him an honorable position over the household of an Egyptian high official named Potiphar. He was given a great deal of power, but Joseph didn't allow temptation to override his responsibility to his master and his God:

Now Joseph was well-built and handsome, and after a while his master's wife took notice of Joseph and said, "Come to bed with me!"

But he refused. "With me in charge," he told her, "my master does not concern himself with anything in the house; everything he owns he has entrusted to my care. No one is greater in this house than I am. My master has withheld nothing from me except you, because you are his wife. How then could I do such a wicked thing and sin against God?" And though she spoke to

Joseph day after day, he refused to go to bed with her or even be with her. (Gen. 39:6–10)

What strength this young man possessed! Joseph knew whom he served—first God and then his master—and he refused to dishonor either of them. Joseph was seventeen years old when he was sold into slavery, so he was probably between twenty-one and twenty-five when he was tempted by Potiphar's wife. But his decision for purity was made long before he was alone with her. He had committed full allegiance and obedience to God and he would not break that vow. Plus, he had the entire household entrusted to him and would not dishonor his earthly master. In a tremendous example of godly character, Joseph lived a righteous life. His life was not governed by spur-of-the-moment decisions or flippant, hormonal emotions. He'd made his choice *before* the encounter to live a pure life for God. Then when he was faced with temptation, he didn't debate himself in the midst of hormones and desire. He already knew the answer.

The story continues: "One day he went into the house to attend to his duties, and none of the household servants was inside. She caught him by his cloak and said, 'Come to bed with me!' But he left his cloak in her hand and ran out of the house" (Gen. 39:11–12). That pesky Potiphar's wife was persistent. No matter how many times Joseph told her no, she would not relent. This time, he literally left his coat and ran. Sometimes, running is the only option left. Toying with the line of temptation is a dangerous practice. Sometimes we simply must run.

MODELING PURITY FOR OUR CHILDREN

A dad went in to pray with his daughter at bedtime. She prayed, "Make me big and strong like my daddy."

He broke down at her words and prayed, "Make me clean and keep me pure like my little girl."

We must certainly model wise choices for our children. Their impressionable minds are watching and soaking up information from observing our lives every day. Are they seeing us watch questionable programs or read inappropriate literature? What about our behavior? Many single parents discourage their teenagers from having sex while they have a boyfriend or girlfriend who often spends the night. What message are those parents sending to their teenagers about their own values? Can we live inconsistent lives and expect our kids to follow principles we are only talking about and not practicing?

How can a young man keep his way pure?
By living according to your word.

—*Psalm 119:9*

Knowing God's Word

One of the safeguards we can place in our lives to protect our purity is to pray and study the Word of God. Psalm 119:11 says, "I have hidden your word in my heart that I might not sin against you." Knowing God's Word helps us to know right and wrong and think on it in times of temptation. If we're "treasuring up" (Matt. 6:20) His Word, then the Holy Spirit can bring it to mind when we need it most. Nothing can be remembered if it's not first learned.

Knowing the Word of God helps us to be victorious in temptation. Look at Jesus' example:

Then Jesus was led by the Spirit into the desert to be tempted by the devil. After fasting forty days and forty nights, he was hungry. The tempter came to him and said, "If you are the Son of God, tell these stones to become bread."

Jesus answered, "It is written: 'Man does not live on bread alone, but on every word that comes from the mouth of God.'"

Then the devil took him to the holy city and had him stand on the highest point of the temple. "If you are the Son of God," he said, "throw yourself down. For it is written: "'He will command his angels concerning you, and they will lift you up in their hands, so that you will not strike your foot against a stone.'"

Jesus answered him, "It is also written: 'Do not put the Lord your God to the test.'"

Again, the devil took him to a very high mountain and showed him all the kingdoms of the world and their splendor. "All this I will give you," he said, "if you will bow down and worship me."

Jesus said to him, "Away from me, Satan! For it is written: 'Worship the Lord your God, and serve him only.'" (Matt. 4:1–10)

LEGACY TRIP IDEA #9
Go fishing, backpacking, dirt bike riding, rock climbing, or horseback riding.

The writer of Hebrews says the Word is "sharper than any double-edged sword" (Heb. 4:12). It can drive away any temptation the Enemy wants to throw at us. But His Word must be stored in our hearts ahead of time to come out when needed. We can't expect to fight such a powerful enemy without weapons. The sword of the Spirit has all the power we need to combat Satan.

Guarding Our Hearts

With the safeguard of God's Word in place, we also need to guard our eyes and ears to protect our mind and heart. Let's call them the "eye-gate" and the "ear-gate." What are we allowing into our brains and hearts through what we watch, read, and listen to? This is another way of thinking about loving God with all our mind. But in this case, we're specifically focusing on sexual purity. God is the only reliable gate-keeper. We're weak human beings. The Enemy knows that and will try to exploit our weaknesses. But if we surrender those areas to the Lord and listen for the Holy Spirit's warnings, we will protect ourselves from the numerous temptations. So it begs the question: Are we allowing those things that are teasing and tantalizing us to replace our true affections?

Jesus said,

> You have heard that it was said, "Do not commit adultery." But I tell you that anyone who looks at a woman lustfully has already committed adultery with her in his heart. If your right eye causes you to sin, gouge it out and throw it away. It is better for you to lose one part of your body than for your whole body to be thrown into hell. And if your right hand causes you to sin, cut it off and throw it away. It is better for you to lose one part of your body than for your whole body to go into hell. (Matt. 5:27–30)

While those are some pretty weighty words, we don't want to hear in the news that adults all over the country are gouging out their eyes or cutting off their hands. The point is that since purity of the mind and body is very important to God, we too should take it seriously. Hear the spirit of the message: Do not let a part of your body affect where your eternal address will be. It's just not worth the sacrifice.

In the Matthew passage, Jesus is talking about both physical and emotional attachment. For men, the physical—specifically the eye-gate—tends to be a problem. Where are we letting our eyes roam? Are we disrespecting someone's wife, mother, or daughter by looking where we shouldn't look and allowing thoughts to form? Pornography is such a horrible temptation for men. But how do you expect to be the spiritual leader in your home if you're in the habit of looking at images that cause you to sin? For women, the problem tends to be emotional. To whom are we becoming emotionally attached—desiring to spend time with and gain respect and compliments from?

Jesus said that if we commit adultery in our heart, we have committed sin. Know that there's a difference between *temptation* and *sin*, but let's also not try to pass over sin as simply "how we are made" or "that's just who we are." God has clearly drawn the line in the sand, and we have no business sidling up to it as close as we can.

Avoiding Temptation

Stay away from tempting environments. The Bible says "Through love and faithfulness sin is atoned for; through the fear of the LORD a man avoids evil . . . The highway of the upright avoids evil; he who guards his way guards his life" (Prov. 16:6, 17). Whereas the eye- and ear-gates help us make decisions on how we will respond to the temptations coming at us *right now*, we can also make a decision to purposefully avoid the *location* of the temptation.

Do you have a problem with online pornography? Then don't allow yourself to *ever* be at a computer alone. We have one friend who gives his wife the modem to the computer if she goes to bed before he does. That's *literally* getting temptation out of the way. Do you have trouble with watching certain movies? Delete those channels from your remote access or even cancel your cable and video membership. Sometimes we become stronger by eliminating the temptation entirely, rather than trying to resist it repeatedly. For most people, avoiding potentially damaging situations in the first place is the best way to defeat sexual temptation. It doesn't make us stronger to stay in an environment and lose than it does to run and win. Why do we like to see how close to the fire we can get before we get burned? Get away! It's like the alcoholic who continues to walk into the bar, sit down with drinks all around him, and determine he will not take a drink. That's ridiculous, right? Stay out of the bar!

Setting Your Resolve

Purity is not always maintained through a conscious refusal to succumb. Sometimes it's through a decision to run. We just have to get out of the situation. But the decision to run must be made *before* the temptation occurs, not during. Face it; our sexual drives are very strong and often override any attempt at rational reasoning. We should determine our resolve in advance. In the moment, when those hormones are raging, we just don't think clearly enough to make wise choices.

Who may ascend the hill of the LORD? Who may stand in his holy place? He who has clean hands and a pure heart, who does not lift up his soul to an idol or swear by what is false. He will receive blessing from the LORD and vindication from God his Savior.
—*Psalm 24:3–5*

We have a married friend (we'll call her Sarah) who was hired for a temporary position at a company. She worked at the same desk as a handsome young man. He soon began to ask personal questions and take an interest in her life. She instantly felt uneasy but was unsure as to what to do, so she asked God to give her an answer. The danger signs loomed in front of her, but should she quit the job she just started an hour ago? It wasn't until she was on an airplane and heard the attendant going through the speech about the "closest exit may be the one behind you" that Sarah realized she had to quit her job. She had to walk out the door that was behind her chair and leave. Sarah really needed the money to pay off mounting debts, but she also knew her marriage simply wasn't worth fourteen dollars an hour. She chose to run. The very next day Sarah was offered another job with comparable pay. God honors our obedience.

Create in me a pure heart, O God, and renew
a steadfast spirit within me.

—*Psalm 51:10*

Being Accountable

After we've read the Word and prayed and turned off the computer and TV, there's one more step to help in our quest for purity. We should be accountable to someone. We need to have someone in our life who can ask the difficult questions. It may be your spouse. I (Jerolyn) can ask Jim any question about how he uses his time. If you don't have a spouse, seek out a friend you trust enough to be honest with, or who will know when you aren't being honest and will call you on it. Give that person permission to pry into your life. Maybe you'll get together a small group of men or women to hold each other accountable. Too many temptations are flying around us every day to think that we can stay pure of our own willpower.

God organizes His church into communities of believers so that people can help each other grow. Often we simply don't want others to know our struggles. There's a risk in sharing openly our secret temptations, but the rewards are greater than the risk. So rely on accountability and trust to help maintain the commitment to remain pure. You can create environments in which you can be honest with yourself and surround yourself with others who will help you live a life of purity.

We can name dozens of people who have waited to have sex until marriage—ourselves included. It's possible to live a life of purity. If you've already surrendered your purity, God can restore you spiritually. Commit to Him to live as He has directed from this day forward. You can make a fresh start with a new resolve to remain pure for His glory and for your good.

TEACHING OUR CHILDREN PURITY

Parents, we must help our kids know how to remain pure and provide the support and boundaries they need to do just that. Create an environment of discussion. Lay down some limitations—TV shows or movies they can't watch, music to avoid, curfews, and dating restrictions. Have discussions about male and female differences in how we respond sexually and what to avoid in a relationship to remain pure. We must provide our kids with safeguards to prevent and protect themselves from sexual temptations.

Be Involved

The politically correct stance seems to be let them be themselves and make their own decisions—"wait till marriage" is deemed too puritanical. The only "protection" talked about today is condoms. But our children are too immature and hormone-driven to make these decisions themselves. If everyone around them is saying it's okay to have sex before marriage, why wouldn't they go that route? It's our job to guide them to right decisions. We must be the voice of reason in their lives. Keep the lines of dialogue open and be honest with your children.

On the Legacy Trip with Shay, as a father and son, he and I (Jim) had a very open discussion about remaining pure. Although the "lesson" was in the morning around the breakfast table at the restaurant, we delved into the discussion with much greater detail as we walked and played golf for eighteen holes. Now, we had "the talk" years ago about sex and sexuality, but this was much more of a young man and older man/dad talking about the things he would be facing in the next few years before and after marriage. It was a great discussion and maybe one you can only have when you are out away from distractions and have specifically set it as a part of the agenda. By the way, we think Shay was a little surprised that his "old man" (no disrespect intended here) knew so much slang, terminology, and information about the subject.

Disciple Them

In protecting our children's purity, it's our responsibility to help them sharpen their sword for battle. Teach them how to study the Word of God and to spend time alone with Him daily. This can start at a very young age. A friend taught us how to train children in having TAWG (Time Alone With God). She began when her children were just able to sit up alone. She would prop them up with pillows and walk out of their eyesight for five minutes. As they got older the time increased, and they were given certain boundaries for the time—read their Bible or a devotional book, listen to Christian music, draw, journal, or play quietly. This has become such a valued time for her children that her young teenagers are up to ninety minutes of TAWG a day. The bottom-line principle here is that since we teach our children how to have good study habits for school, we can't neglect teaching them how to learn from the Word of God. It takes study and discipline. Train them.

Establish Guidelines

While we can guide our children to the Word that is their source of power, we also need to train them to take control of those things that will try to control them. If they don't, the Enemy will. Help your children to guard their eyes and ears. Their bodies

LEGACY TRIP IDEA #10

Go to see one of the world's great symphonies or art museums.

are the temple of God, so they must be taught how to guard the temple and keep it pure. They don't always know when to turn off TVs, stereos, or computers. But you do, so do it. We can't just let them run free with a computer, TV, and stereo in their room with the door shut. If one of your children has an especially strong weakness in this area, you must keep them away from the things that cause them to succumb to their temptation. Know what your children are listening to and watching; with whom they're with chatting online. For example, MySpace and Facebook are popular social Web sites for teens. We have every right as parents to get their user names and passwords and periodically check the sites they visit to see what they are saying to others and what others are saying to them. Kids also upload pictures to these sites. What is your teenager looking at? Many teens are now sending provocative pictures of themselves to others online or by cell phone. Checking their Facebook or cell phone is not an invasion of their privacy, as some people would like to espouse. It's our parental responsibility.

PRACTICAL IDEAS FOR TEACHING PURITY

All Ages

- Talk to your children about their bodies being the temple of God.
- Teach them about appropriate touch and not to play with their bodies.
- Teach them to respect other people's bodies. Do not touch other's private parts.
- Honestly answer their questions about their bodies. Give only as much information as needed.

Ages 6–10

- Explain sex to your children when you feel they are ready to learn about it. Kids will usually start asking questions around intimacy. There are wonderful Christian books that explain sex in a very appropriate way and stress that sex is only for marriage. Your kids are going to learn about sex. Better from you than someone else.
- Never leave boys and girls alone in a room with the door closed. They are very curious and will explore.

Ages 11–17

- Encourage modest choices in clothing. Girls especially may be tempted to choose clothing that reveals too much of their developing bodies. Explain to them the reasons for modesty.
- Establish dating restrictions: age, curfew, where they can go, and who they can go with.
- Encourage group dating. There's safety in numbers.
- Spend as much time with your teenager's special someone as they do. Have them in your home as much as possible.
- Help your child establish an accountability partner—someone they can be open and honest with and who will ask tough questions. It could be you, but in most cases it will be someone else. Direct your child to a pastor, a teacher, or a youth sponsor rather than another teenager. Help them choose someone who is wise and dependable that you and your child both trust.
- Teach your children to recognize compromising situations and to run from them. Once they start dating, establish a code system where they can reach out to you for help without embarrassment with their friends. If they are in an uncomfortable situation, they can use the code to let you know, and you can come get them.

continued

PRACTICAL IDEAS FOR TEACHING PURITY

All Ages

- Help your child learn to guard the "eye-gate" and the "ear-gate."
- Check what music your children are listening to. Check their CDs and MP3 players. Print out the words to the songs and discuss the lyrics. Allow in your home only music you approve.
- Control what your kids are watching on TV, at the movies, and on the computer.
  - Movies: Visit www.kidsinmind.com or http://www.pluggedinonline.com/ from Focus on the Family.
  - Computer: Check their Internet history. Use protective software to make it impossible for them to visit certain sites.
  - Social Internet sites, like MySpace and Facebook: Check who they are talking to and what they are talking about. Also, check who they are sharing pictures with and what those pictures are.

Hold Them Accountable

We need to be the parent and make the tough decisions for ourselves and for our children to protect them from the evils thrown at them every day. Explain to them what is happening in their bodies and why they have these temptations. God designed our teens with these desires; we just need to help them understand those urgings and teach them how to build self-control through boundaries in their lives. God designed this plan for their good. Joe McIlhaney and Freda McKissic Bush, in their book *Hooked: New Science on How Casual Sex Is Affecting Our Children*, state that when adolescents have sex, a chemical reaction occurs in the brain that affects their decision making later in life. It states that teenagers' "brains actually can come to perceive dangerous and unhealthy behavior—like sleeping with one partner after another—as normal. And this can damage the brain's emotional bonding mechanism, making it difficult for a teenager to form healthy, long-term relationships in the future."[1] The problems of adolescent sex are no longer just a "Christian" issue. The scientific community is beginning to recognize the dangers this activity has on teenagers' physical well-being, as well as their emotional and relational stability.

What goes into a man's mouth does not make him "unclean,"
but what comes out of his mouth, that is what makes him "unclean" . . .
Don't you see that whatever enters the mouth goes into the stomach
and then out of the body? But the things that come out of the mouth
come from the heart, and these make a man "unclean."

—*Matthew 15:11, 17–18*

We've talked with our kids about making the decision to abstain before the moment of temptation occurs. Keep clear, open dialogue going with your children so they know they can ask questions and trust you with their struggles in the area of sexual temptations. In this way, you will become your child's accountability partner. We often ask our dating children, "How are you doing in remaining pure?" Because we've built a relationship and history on truth, we know they will be honest with us. If you question your child's honesty, maybe some stricter curfews and stipulations need to be established. We encourage group dating or spending time at our house, so they are placed in less tempting situations. Our child's "special someone" needs to spend more time with us and less time alone with our child. We need to be the parents in the most loving way we can and train our children to protect their purity.

If your child is uncomfortable talking to you about sexual struggles, encourage him or her to ask an older, responsible Christian to be an accountability partner and mentor who will answer questions. As the parent, we have every right to choose or approve who that mentor will be. Guide your children to choose wisely someone who will help them strengthen their resolve. Just as we need accountability, we need to help our children have the same environment in which they can grow.

Even in this day of sexual openness and freedoms, we're not being idealistic when we say that our sons and daughters can remain virgins till marriage. We have a responsibility to lead our children to live a life of purity for God and for their future spouse.

QUESTION AND GIFT

The purity gift is a ring worn on the left hand, to be replaced only by an engagement ring or wedding ring. There are True Love Waits rings you can purchase from any Christian book store. We chose, however, to pick a special ring designed with each child's taste in mind. It's one they can give to their spouse on their wedding day or keep and wear on their right hand. Maybe your child would rather wear a bracelet or necklace as the reminder.

If your child does not want to wear jewelry, there are written covenants he or she can sign. (Go to www.truelovewaits.com.) The main point—with a ring or with a signed covenant—is that our child is reminded that he or she is married to Christ alone at this point in life and must remain pure for his or her future spouse. The world has a dozen other ways to initiate our children into this time of sexual awareness, but marriage is the only biblical way. Make it special and memorable as you celebrate your child's passage into a new stage of life.

The question for this value is "What's on your hand?" As with anything we get used to having around, we can forget about a ring or take it for granted. Remind your child periodically why he or she is wearing this ring. We're not being nosy or naggers; we're being parents. Bring the ring and their commitment back to their consciousness so they will continue to make the right choices in their pastimes and relationships.

Not only does God hear, but He also offers hope, help, and answers.
His heart breaks with yours, and He holds out hands of love, grace,
mercy, forgiveness, healing, peace, rest, joy, and compassion.
He promises to renew, restore, rebuild, and reward.

—*Barbara Wilson*

*Lord, my body is Your home, and I want to treat it as Your temple.
Guard my eyes and ears from the temptations that bombard me
every day. Give me the self-discipline to avoid situations that
may tempt me and to run from full-on assaults. Protect my child
from the world's values and help me to provide protection from
the consequences of choosing purity in today's world. Help me to
train my children to guard their purity and their bodies for the
joys of marriage to come, out of respect for themselves, others,
and You. Amen.*

six

POSITIVE ATTITUDE

Gift: Eagle
Question: How high will you fly?

When Jan woke up, the room was frigid. Frost coated the inside of the bedroom window. She wasn't able to pay the heating bill again this month, and there wasn't much hope in meeting next month's obligations. They would just have to make it through.

Jan heard her ten-year-old daughter, Mandy, moving around in the other room getting ready for school. Her heart ached for the suffering Mandy had to endure because of what Jan considered her inadequacies as a provider for her family. Pretty soon, the cute little blonde popped her head around the corner. "Morning, Mom. Remember, I have to be at school early today for the pageant practice."

"Come snuggle with your mama for a minute," Jan said, scooting over and lifting the covers for Mandy to join her. "I'm sorry it's so cold in the apartment. Were you able to sleep?"

"Sure, Mom," Mandy said with a dismissive wave. "I just put on an extra pair of pajamas and socks and snuggled up to my old stuffed animals. I was fine." Jan buried her tear-streaked face in her precious daughter's hair.

UNDERSTANDING POSITIVE ATTITUDE

In a world of war, hunger, fear, unemployment, negative sound bites, broken marriages, and feelings of hopelessness, we are convinced now more than ever of the importance of a positive attitude in our personal lives and in our relationships with others. A positive attitude can lighten the darkest moments. A bad attitude makes us discouraged and unproductive, while a positive attitude moves us forward. Besides, no one wants to be around someone who only wants to complain, gossip, and whine about life. We have often jokingly said of this value, "Our kids will have a positive attitude even if it kills us!"

While some children may naturally have a more positive attitude than others, having an optimistic outlook is a choice. For some, the carnal nature they're born with may tempt them strongly toward the negative. When the Enemy attempts to instill dissatisfaction, which is the root of all sin, they become unhappy with how things are now and try to change their circumstance. If they're unable to change it, they'll be appeased with groaning about their situation.

But if we choose a positive attitude, our thoughts and actions automatically put us in a Christlike frame of thinking and thus affect how we approach and react to life and its ever-changing and challenging circumstances. Someone has said, "Life is 10 percent what happens and 90 percent how I react to it." How we respond to life makes all the difference.

Francie Baltazar-Schwartz tells the story of working with a certain restaurant manager. Jerry was always positive. No matter what hit him, he never showed a negative attitude. Francie asked him one day how he could always be so positive. Jerry replied,

> Each morning I wake up and say to myself, "Jerry, you have two choices today. You can choose to be in a good mood or you can choose to be in a bad mood." I choose to be in a good mood. Each time something bad happens, I can choose to be a victim or I can choose to learn from it. I choose to learn from it. Every time someone comes to me complaining, I can choose to accept their complaining or I can point out the positive side of life. I choose the positive side of life.[1]

There is little difference in people, but that little difference makes a big difference. The little difference is attitude. The big difference is whether it is positive or negative.

—*W. Clement Stone*

A few years after working with Jerry, Francie heard of a tragic turn of events for Jerry. One day when he opened the restaurant, he broke a cardinal rule. He left the back door open. Jerry was held at gunpoint, and when the robbers got spooked, they shot Jerry. As he was lying there on the floor, he thought, *I can choose to live or I can choose to die. I choose to live.* But once he reached the hospital, he saw the despair in the eyes of the doctors and nurses. He decided he had to change the course they were taking. A big, burly nurse asked him if he was allergic to anything and Jerry said, "Yes, bullets." Over their laughter Jerry said, "I am choosing to live. Operate on me as if

I am alive, not dead." And he lived. Attitude choices can make all the difference in the world for our own lives and for the lives of the people we influence. If we choose a positive attitude, we will not only make our own life better and more productive, but we will have an impact on how other people choose to live. Your attitude can make a difference.

The pessimist sees difficulty in every opportunity.
The optimist sees the opportunity in every difficulty.

—*Winston Churchill*

Attitude affects both how you respond and to what heights your response will take you. Lou Holtz, former Notre Dame football coach, said, "Ability is what you are capable of doing. Motivation determines what you do. Attitude determines how well you do it." Everyone is given talents by the Creator. What we do with them is largely determined by who or what motivates us. But even if we have a positive motivator, we will not go very far unless we have a positive attitude to direct us in an unstoppable, upward motion toward excellence.

When hiring new employees, businesses today first look at character, then they consider how a person will fit into the team's chemistry or culture. The most talented people in the world are useless if they have a bad attitude. It's interesting that society is finally learning that, while it is definitely important, competency is much less critical than character and a positive attitude. It seems that our culture is realizing that we can teach people *how*, but we can't teach people *heart*.

THE POSITIVE ATTITUDE OF PAUL

How can a person be tortured, imprisoned, starved, and naked, but possess an attitude above reproach? The apostle Paul did. We believe Paul represents the value of positive attitude as well as anyone else. He walked through so many trials and extreme difficulties after he began his ministry that no one would fault him if he had been negative. However, Paul displayed a level of determination, dedication, and desire we can all learn from.

Determination is, by definition, forbidding anything to stop you; pressing on through the difficulties and obstacles; seeing new problems as opportunities, not dead ends. Paul wrote, "But we have this treasure in jars of clay to show that this all-surpassing power is from God and not from us. We are hard pressed on every side, but not crushed; perplexed, but not in despair; persecuted, but not abandoned; struck down, but not destroyed" (2 Cor. 4:7–9). Remember what Paul's life had looked like up to the point of his writing this? He had not only been persecuted, but even spent some time in prison! And not some nice government-regulated facility with giant-screen color TVs and top-of-the-line workout rooms. This was a dungeon prison—the dark, dank, rat-infested, nightmare kind. What did Paul say about it? He was not crushed, in despair, abandoned, or destroyed. Talk about a positive attitude! You can't have a more extreme viewpoint than Paul's attitude compared to his situation.

Paul's attitude, however, was not drummed up under stress. It was determined long before he faced any trials. He had first chosen an attitude of complete dedication to the Lord and His service. This takes us back to the first core value: devotion. Because Paul had determined long before that his complete devotion was to the Lord, he didn't allow his current circumstances to become attitude-destroyers. He treated them as mere inconveniences. In fact, Paul's positive attitude allowed him to see his trials as a blessing. He said,

> Therefore we do not lose heart. Though outwardly we are wasting away, yet inwardly we are being renewed day by day. For our light and momentary troubles are achieving for us an eternal glory that far outweighs them all. So we fix our eyes not on what is seen, but on what is unseen. For what is seen is temporary, but what is unseen is eternal. (2 Cor. 4:16–18)

Paul lived with an eternal perspective, not a temporal despair. He is saying that what we've experienced is nothing compared to what is to come. We can endure all this for Christ because eternity with Him will make any suffering we have here worthwhile.

A few years ago, we heard Pastor Wayne Cordeiro speak at a leadership conference. He said if we could stretch a rope out in front of us that went for eternity to our left and for eternity to our right, it would represent all time. Then we take a knife and make a little nick in the rope; this is our life on the timeline of eternity. We have such little time here and we're so insignificant. Yet we spend hours of time worrying about and chasing after self-preservation, self-promotion, and recreation. Paul had a much clearer perspective. He said that because time is short, we should devote it to God's service. This is the attitude Christ wants us to exhibit. We're not to spend time whining about our situation or circumstances, which we were either born into or created on our own. Rise above them and serve the Lord, for time is short.

Without a doubt, Paul had an attitude of determination and dedication; he did not serve half-heartedly. He had desire and he knew how to be passionate about his beliefs. Paul's passion was reaching people for Jesus Christ: "Though I am free and belong to no man, I make myself a slave to everyone, to win as many as possible" (1 Cor. 9:19). His one and only desire—above any thought of himself—was to see people change their eternal address from hell to heaven through Jesus Christ. Only a passion to a higher calling could take Paul through what he had to endure. Listen to his heart:

> Rather, as servants of God we commend ourselves in every way: in great endurance; in troubles, hardships and distresses; in beatings, imprisonments and riots; in hard work, sleepless nights and hunger; in purity, understanding, patience and kindness; in the Holy Spirit and in sincere love; in truthful speech and in the power of God; with weapons of righteousness in the right hand and in the left; through glory and dishonor, bad report and good report; genuine, yet regarded as imposters; known, yet regarded as unknown; dying, and yet we live on; beaten, and yet not killed; sorrowful, yet always rejoicing; poor, yet making many rich; having nothing, and yet possessing everything. (2 Cor. 6:4–10)

Paul possessed such a rich positive attitude that he displayed through his determination, dedication, and desire to please the Father in every area of his life. He took the good and the bad in complete balance. Paul would not let anything disrupt his mission for Jesus Christ. It was the very foundation he stood upon. If we can just capture an ounce of his eternal-perspective way of facing life and its trials, we could conquer anything that comes at us.

LEGACY TRIP IDEA #11
Take a bike-riding tour, starting from your home. This is a very cost-effective trip and doesn't require you to fly or drive anywhere!

MODELING POSITIVE ATTITUDE FOR OUR CHILDREN

So how do we instill a positive attitude in ourselves? Many verses throughout the Bible address how to have a positive attitude. Romans 12:2 says, "Do not conform any longer to the pattern of this world, but be transformed by the renewing of your mind. Then you will be able to test and approve what God's will is—his good, pleasing and perfect will." Ephesians 4:22–24 tells us, "You were taught, with regard to your former way of life, to put off your old self, which is being corrupted by its deceitful desires; to be made new in the attitude of your minds; and to put on the new self, created to be like God in true righteousness and holiness." And 2 Corinthians 5:17 says, "Therefore, if anyone is in Christ, he is a new creation; the old has gone, the new has come!"

LEGACY TRIP IDEA #12
Take a camping trip. You can visit a variety of locations, spend tons of time together, and find lots to see, all in close proximity to your home.

Christ is the transforming power to elevate our attitude to a new level. He's provided us with an avenue of redemption from our former way of life to a new outlook. We no longer have to wallow in the muck of sin and darkness—those choices that bring us down to our base level that will only lead to destruction. We're filled with the Spirit of the Almighty and can live a new, transformed life. But salvation is not an instantaneous, permanent, extreme makeover of our actions and attitudes. Our will and hard work is necessary for the changes to occur.

Daily Commitment

First, we must commit to work on our attitude each day with thanksgiving: "Commit to the LORD whatever you do, and your plans will succeed" (Prov. 16:3). Wake up each morning asking the Lord of Lords to guard your attitude. Then, at least once each day, give thanks. Set an alarm to remind you until this habit is ingrained in the DNA of your life. As we continue to practice this new habit, we will find ways to thank Him multiple times throughout the day—even for the bad things that occur, because we realize that God's perspective is superior to ours. The events in our lives happen for a purpose higher than we can discern. So we must trust the Father to guide us through those events and be thankful for His presence. Living in a state of gratitude will move our thinking to a whole new level. Thanksgiving will change our perspective and empower us to move forward, rather than being paralyzed by fear, regret, restlessness, or dead ends.

Positive Friends

Second, we should surround ourselves with positive people. We can't always choose whom we work with, but we can choose our friends. We can select positive ones, who will lift up our thinking and support our attitude to rise above difficult circumstances and trials. Surround yourself with people who uphold a can-do attitude, rather than living in doubt and defeat. Through them, we'll experience and grow in a positive attitude that can displace the negative thoughts and words we previously relied on.

As for negative coworkers, we can make it a project to turn their negativism to a positive bent. We should never give them the power to bring us down to their level; by doing so we're only succumbing to our old sinful nature. Instead, we can live exemplary lives that challenge them to raise their own focus to new heights. We can adjust our perspective so that we are no longer influenced by negative people, but instead become a positive influence ourselves.

If positive thinking is a struggle, surround yourself with crowds of positive people. Their attitude tends to be contagious. Consciously choose to hang out in locations where positive people reside. Become involved in activities with positive people. Invite friends to your home who will lift you and others up. Hearing that kind of positive perspective throughout your conversations will reinforce positive primary reactions to whatever life throws at you. Positive people help to mold other positive people and everyone is lifted up to a new height. Remember the saying: You can't soar with the eagles when you hang around the turkeys.

Renewed Mind

Now that we have placed ourselves in a positive position—spiritually and physically—it's time to evaluate our thought processes. Ask yourself, "Do I look at everything in a negative light? Is my first thought an 'I can't' reaction? If so, why?" If we know the origin of our thinking, we can address the root issue. Were you raised by negative parents or guardians? Do you really want to continue that legacy? Have you experienced failures in the past that have influenced your thinking on the future? Determine where your negativity was spawned, acknowledge the source, and then ask God to replace it or transform it. This may take some time, because roots can grow deep and hold fast. But if we're going to choose to continue building a healthy, productive legacy for our children, root cancers must be destroyed before they infect our offspring. God's healing power can make amazing changes in our outlook on life if we let it. We don't have to live in generational defeat or adolescent-learned practices. Our childhood doesn't have to own us. We can start a new pattern through the power of Jesus Christ that overcomes those learned habits and creates new, healthier ones.

Our personal transformation to a positive attitude continues by practicing "I can" rather than "I can't" thinking. We can do anything we set our minds to do. We may not do it perfectly or even as well as the next guy, but we can do it if we put our minds and effort into it.

We're the children of the I Am who can do it all. "I can do everything through him who gives me strength" (Phil. 4:13). Deny the defeatist attitude that the Enemy will tempt you to take. He has no power over you that you do not give to him. With God's guidance and strength and our little bit of faith and a right attitude, the possibilities grow exponentially.

Spiritual Reading

Another way to continue on an upward path is by reading. Scripture should always be first. The Word of God doesn't promote any negative or discouraging thoughts—always a right attitude. The Spirit of the Father can use His Word to inspire and direct our thinking with more power than we can ever drum up for ourselves. It's a positive attitude that begins in the heart and works its way out to our thoughts and actions. But other inspiring books will help as well. Many Christian authors, both classic and contemporary, will direct our thinking to the awesome power of living in Christ and help pull us out of the Enemy's trap of negativity.

Ninety percent of the game is half mental.
—*Yogi Berra*

All of these processes can work only by our choosing the right attitude as an act of our will. Our kids are watching to see which choices we make. One evening we were having a family dinner time and a subject was brought up that I (Jim) didn't like. I proceeded to complain about it and tried to couch my objection in a "nice" manner.

Well into my objection, Gabby said, "Dad, you are the one always talking about being positive, but that doesn't sound like a positive attitude." Busted! Ouch! The guy who "preaches" to his kids and tries to live it out was allowing himself to be negative. Even in our attempts, it's a challenge for all of us, no matter how positive we are—or maybe think we are. We're faced with the challenge of keeping it positive. Yes, we can complain, and yes, we can be "concerned," but how we come across to others speaks volumes about our attitude. A positive attitude is a choice. What choice are you making?

No one can force our attitude—for good or for bad. The choice lies completely in our hands. Choose to look at the glass half full, not half empty. Choose to see life as possibilities, not obstacles. Even if you've been abused or raised in a negative environment, you can break the pattern. Choose to no longer live your life as a victim, carrying an attitude you feel you have a right to hang on to. You're only making your life miserable. Make the decision to view life in a positive light. Life will not be all rosy colored and sweet—nobody's life is. But our attitude toward our circumstances will start us off on a stronger plane. Not every obstacle we face is a roadblock. Sometimes it can become an interesting detour.

We must approach life with a positive attitude so we are acting like we want our children to act. Parents, we're often the ones to blame when our children have a negative response to life. How many times have horrible prejudices and false philosophies been passed down from generation to generation, poisoning the very ones we love? Our attitudes will make a difference in the lives of our children. Let's analyze our own approach to life and then model a positive attitude for our kids—a legacy we hope they will choose to embrace. It's not too late to begin.

TEACHING OUR CHILDREN POSITIVE ATTITUDE

"Train a child in the way he should go, and when he is old he will not turn from it" (Prov. 22:6). Our children's positive attitudes are not going to develop automatically. Like many other important habits, it'll take some time and training. They'll learn many of these habits by mimicking us, but they all need to be intentionally reinforced through training and practice.

Affirm Them

We can begin to help our children with a positive attitude by affirming them for who they are and not just what they do. We should tell them how proud we are of them, simply because they are our kids. We love to sneak up on one of our kids and tell them we love them and that we're very proud of them—for no reason at all. This often leads into a great time of snuggling and laughing. We do praise our kids over and over when they do something well in sports, drama, or academics. But the deeper, lasting compliments will shape who they are and make them more positive about themselves and their world. If you or your children aren't snugglers, find your children's love languages—how they best receive love and praise—and "speak" their language to them. A little extra time and effort will reap tremendous returns in your children's attitudes.

A wonderful book to read is *The Five Love Languages* by Gary Chapman. This is a great resource that helps us to determine how we receive love and how others receive love. The basic premise is that if love is given to a person in their love language, it will have a greater, lasting impact. If we affirm our children for who they are, just as God made them, we will establish a strong foundation on which to build a positive attitude about life. In addition to loving our children just for who they are and praising their accomplishments,

PRACTICAL IDEAS FOR TEACHING *POSITIVE ATTITUDE*

All Ages

- When your child demonstrates a good attitude in a tough situation, give praise.

Ages 2–5

- Start your child's day with Scripture. Children can learn simple verses that place positive thoughts in their minds.
- Discourage the use of the words, "I can't."

Ages 6–10

- Send your child to school with a positive comment, like "Choose to make it a great day."
- Help your child develop a positive self-image. Praise your children, not just for what they do, but also for who they are.
- Don't let your children get the "give me" bug. Be sure they are thankful for each privilege they receive before they get another one.
- Help your kids choose good friends. Observe their friends, and if you see an attitude problem in a child, discuss it later with your child. Determine if their friend's attitude is influencing your child or if your child is being a good influencer. Either way, set up boundaries and checkpoints in their relationship. For example, if you see bad attitudes after your child has been with a friend, you might restrict them from being together for a while.
- Explain to your daughters (at around nine years old) about hormones, and the affect they have on their attitudes. Help them establish a plan for dealing with them.

Ages 11–17

- Discuss with your boys the affects of hormones on their attitude. Help them establish a plan for dealing with them.
- Teach your children how to present an opposing viewpoint without being negative or disrespectful. They are stretching their wings and opinions; let them grow in an appropriate way.
- Even if an attitude of respect has been established in the home, it will be challenged during the teen years. Do not allow inappropriate words or attitudes. Parents are still the authority and must maintain control over the home. But we parents must also show our children respect.

continued

PRACTICAL IDEAS FOR TEACHING *POSITIVE ATTITUDE*

Parents

- What words are your children hearing come out of your mouth—positive or negative? We set the tone of the home and are the primary example to our children on how we will choose to view life.
- Establish an attitude of thanksgiving in your home.

we also need to applaud them for doing things right. We should tell them they did well when they have a good attitude in a tough situation. What about when they treat their sibling in a loving manner or do their chores without complaining? Maybe they set the table without being asked or told someone they were sorry for an offense they committed without our stepping in and demanding the apology. All these positive attitudes and actions need to be recognized and immediately reinforced with praise.

All people desire recognition and praise. Humans are inherently insecure and need awards and encouragement to continue to press forward. We, as parents, never want to be found speaking *only* instruction and criticism to our children. Give them the respect due them when they've done well. Encourage their good behavior. It's also a really nice break from the negative aspect of consequences for misbehavior and promotes a more positive attitude in us as well. Praise and recognition take such little time but make such a huge impact.

Reinforcing Positive Attitudes

While we are helping our children establish a positive self-image, we can help them work on positive attitude habits. When confronted with a new challenge, our kids will often start with "I can't." We stop them right there every time. They're declaring failure before they have even tried. That attitude is unacceptable in our house. We then talk through the "I can" possibilities. Eventually, they come around to attempt whatever challenge is placed before them. If we had allowed the "I can'ts" to win, our children's attitude toward new situations would habitually be negative. When we reinforce "I can" thinking, they'll eventually begin each new opportunity with a positive perspective.

Develop Grateful Hearts

Another way to reinforce positive attitudes in our children is through encouraging thankfulness. For example, our kids can struggle with being thankful for a special outing we have just taken. Have you ever been walking out of a movie theater or picking your child up from an overnight with a friend and the first thing out of their mouth is, "Can we go out to eat?" or "I want to call so and so to come over and play." We've had that happen too many times. Our children are growing up in such an entertainment-oriented society that there's something fun and exciting available to do at all hours of the day. So they start to develop an amusement-park mentality. They finish one fun thing and expect us to have another one waiting. Sort of like getting off one roller coaster and hustling over to the next bigger and faster one. These are the moments to teach our children to stop and be thankful for what they have just experienced and not immediately search hungrily for the next exciting event.

Meet Their Friends

Just as we need to be careful about whom we're spending time with, we also need to watch whom our kids are hanging out with and who is influencing their attitudes. We like to encourage our kids to have their friends come to our house so we can observe their behaviors and conversations.

Then later, if we have concerns with those friends, we can talk to our children about the influences they're allowing into their lives. Most of the time, our children won't choose to hang out with bad influencers. But if they don't make the right choices, we, as parents, have a responsibility to do it for them. We always hope our children are strong enough to be positive influencers no matter who they're with. But there may be stages in their lives when they are not mature enough to make that call, and we'll need to control whom we allow into their circle of influence.

Yet this I call to mind and therefore I have hope: Because of the LORD's great love we are not consumed, for his compassions never fail. They are new every morning; great is your faithfulness.
—*Lamentations 3:21–23*

We need to mention something here about adolescent hormones. They wreak havoc on our children's attitudes. Just plan on it. Beginning at around age nine for a girl and about age twelve for a boy, we must have exemplary patience to ease our children through this difficult time. Be sure they understand what's going on with their bodies and that their feelings are natural and not their fault. Make some plans for when they are having "bad" days. They should never be allowed to cross the line of respect, but they may need more coddling through this stage. Most of the problems will surface in their attitude, so work them into another mood through play, change of location, exercise, a nap, whatever works. Our households will be much more peaceful if *we* have the right attitude about their growing pains.

QUESTION AND GIFT

Our gift for the positive attitude core value is an eagle figurine. The question that goes with it is "How high will you fly?" A negative attitude will keep us crawling among the thistles, but positive thinking will help us soar above the treetops. It's all a matter of perspective and choice. We want to soar, and we want our children to soar as well.

Lord, there is so much negativity around us. Our tendency is to fall into that trap when events of life do not go as planned. Help me to see life with Your eyes and Your perspective. Protect my heart from the dark attitudes that the Enemy plants. Guide me to demonstrate and inspire my child to fly high with a positive attitude and glorify You in every situation. Amen.

seven

GENEROSITY

Gift: Dollar bill or silver dollar
Question: How are you doing with what you hold?

L ast night I (Jerolyn) awoke from a dream with a very heavy and disturbed heart. A large group of children had come to our church and were paraded down the aisles. In the normal confusion and blur of a dream, I didn't hear why these children were there. Since they carried little pictures and stickers, I thought they must be selling them to raise money for some project. Pulling out a dollar bill, I reached into the aisle past one of the adults leading the children to hand it to a little girl passing by. The eyes of the adult locked onto mine and froze the dream. In that moment I knew this was not some small project that needed a few spare dollars, but one that required great generosity to help relieve the depths of the children's despair. The woman's eyes spoke so many messages at once—incredulity, pain, pleading, judgment exposing my stinginess, shame in the knowledge that she was a fellow human being with so little compassion. As I lay in bed, contemplating the meaning of this dream, I was faced with the question—"Do I have a generous heart toward others and thus toward God, or am I trying to hold on to as much for myself as possible, with only small, gratuitous, charitable gestures now and then?"

UNDERSTANDING GENEROSITY

Our money and our time take up a great deal of our energy as we seek after more and more. We try to take as little time as possible to make more money, so we can have more stuff and do more fun things. Isn't this the basic philosophy today—at least in the US? How can I make more money, but have more time to play? This thinking could not be further removed from a Christlike attitude. Jesus, who had very little money, gave of His time to hurting people who needed to hear the truth. If we're to become more like Christ and have a spiritually vital life, then we must practice generosity as Christ did and teach our children to be just as generous.

What exactly does generosity look like? Paul gives a wonderful illustration of generosity as he shares about the activities of the Macedonian churches:

And now, brothers, we want you to know about the grace that God has given the Macedonian churches. Out of the most severe trial, their overflowing joy and their extreme poverty welled up in rich generosity. For I testify that they gave as much as they were able, and even beyond their ability. Entirely on their own, they urgently pleaded with us for the privilege of sharing in this service to the saints. And they did not do as we expected, but they gave themselves first to the Lord and then to us in keeping with God's will. So we urged Titus, since he had earlier made a beginning, to bring also to completion this act of grace on your part. But just as you excel in everything—in faith, in speech, in knowledge, in complete earnestness and in your love for us—see that you also excel in this grace of giving.

I am not commanding you, but I want to test the sincerity of your love by comparing it with the earnestness of others. For you know the grace of our Lord Jesus Christ, that though he was rich, yet for your sakes he became poor, so that you through his poverty might become rich.

And here is my advice about what is best for you in this matter: Last year you were the first not only to give but also to have the desire to do so. Now finish the work, so that your eager willingness to do it may be matched by your completion of it, according to your means. For if the willingness is there, the gift is acceptable according to what one has, not according to what he does not have.

Our desire is not that others might be relieved while you are hard pressed, but that there might be equality. At the present time your plenty will supply what they need, so that in turn their plenty will supply what you need. Then there will be equality, as it is written: "He who gathered much did not have too much, and he who gathered little did not have too little." (2 Cor. 8:1–15)

Do all the good you can; By all the means you can;
In all the ways you can; In all the places you can; At all the times
you can; To all the people you can; As long as ever you can.

—*John Wesley*

Generosity is not a disposition; it's a decision. Look back at the first couple of verses. The churches had severe trials. It doesn't say just a few difficulties, but severe trials. Yet out of their extreme poverty they gave what they had. And—look closely, this is very important—they gave in their overflowing joy. They weren't giving grudgingly, saying, "We have nothing; how do they expect us to help others? Are we to take food out of our children's mouths to feed their children?" Rather, in their overflowing joy in giving even in their extreme poverty they demonstrated amazing generosity. They even pleaded urgently for the privilege of giving. The Macedonians made a decision beyond what their base temperament of protecting self would dictate. In our human nature, we seek self-preservation above all else. The Macedonians, however, chose to help others even with the little they had and did it joyfully. Second Corinthians 9:7 says, "Each man should give what he has decided in his heart to give, not reluctantly or under compulsion, for God loves a cheerful giver." We must fight our self-preserving tendencies and choose to share with a Christlike attitude of the heart with joy.

If you can't feed a hundred people, then just feed one.
—*Mother Teresa*

Once we decide to give, our generosity meets needs and blesses us. Second Corinthians 9:8 says, "And God is able to make all grace abound to you, so that in all things at all times, having all that you need, you will abound in every good work." When we open ourselves up to others with our finances and with our time, we may think we are blessing them, but we're actually the ones blessed. It happens every time.

Last Christmas, our church partnered with a local organization to host a Christmas party for underprivileged children in our area. Through generous donations and the help of a local store, we were able to give away sixty bicycles to the children who attended. Watching their stunned expressions when all those bikes rolled into the room was priceless. As the emcee called their names to go get their bikes, we could see a change come over their faces. It took several moments to sink in, but they finally realized those bikes were really for them, and then the smiles overflowed. One tearful mother later told a volunteer, "My son has been asking for a bicycle. We've only been in the country for a few months and thought we would never be able to afford to get him one. Thank you so much for making my son's dream come true." We'd never seen so many happy children riding bikes around one room or so many incredulous smiles. This wasn't just Christmas for those families; it was Christmas for us too. We experienced the joy of the celebration through their eyes. God never lets us empty our coffers without filling them with something far better. He is so faithful when we're faithful to be His hands, feet, and wallet.

Generosity also communicates our love for God and glorifies Him with thanksgiving. "Now he who supplies seed to the sower and bread for food will also supply and increase your store of seed and will enlarge the harvest of your righteousness. You will be made rich in every way so that you can be generous on every occasion, and through us your generosity will result in thanksgiving to God" (2 Cor. 9:10–11). As we serve, we supply the needs of God's people, who then pour out expressions of thanks to God. He delights in our generosity, because when it's done with a cheerful heart and out of unselfish motives, He is glorified.

THE GENEROSITY OF BARNABAS

When looking throughout the Scriptures for someone demonstrating the character of generosity, Barnabas, an early church missionary, was a name that continued to surface. But we wondered if he was the best choice. Traditionally, Barnabas is associated more with relationships, calling, and development of people, rather than generosity. But as we searched the Scriptures further, it became clear that he demonstrates all those characteristics *because* of his generous spirit. Generosity leads the way in how Barnabas, whose name means "Encourager," advanced God's kingdom. We see it in his finances, belief in others, and his grace—generosity at its best! Although we don't know a great deal about Barnabas, a portrait of his values is found in a few different passages.

Acts 4:37 says Barnabas "sold a field he owned and brought the money and put it at the apostles' feet." People with a generous spirit will usually display that characteristic in all areas of their lives through grace, love, forgiveness, encouragement, and beliefs, to name a few. But finances are often the tangible way we see generosity demonstrated. In Acts 4, Barnabas is not the only one who gives away his profits for others to benefit, but he is the only one mentioned by name. Speculation is that his field may have been of significant size and value, and he gave the whole amount from the sale of this property. Barnabas's lack of hesitancy demonstrates a heart completely engaged with the Master and willing to give generously to serve Him. How often do we piecemeal out to the Father our dutiful contribution, as we place a dollar or two in the offering plate? Barnabas gave it all because he knew whose it was. He generously worshiped the Lord with his wallet.

Barnabas was very generous with his money, but he was also generous with his trust in people. "When [Paul] came to Jerusalem, he tried to join the disciples, but they were all afraid of him, not believing that he really was a disciple" (Acts 9:26). So Barnabas took Paul under his care and defended his trustworthiness to the disciples. Paul was well known to them from his days of attacking and imprisoning Christ's followers. Who could be sure of his authenticity in being transformed by Christ and his potential as an agent of change for Christ and His cause? The disciples certainly were skeptical. They weren't ready to hand over the keys to the Kingdom and blindly believe that Paul was honestly now on

LEGACY TRIP IDEA #13
Find an opportunity locally or within driving distance to volunteer at a nonprofit or ministry organization

their side. They struggled with unconditionally receiving him, and understandably so. Paul was a man who had actively tried to have them imprisoned. He had demonstrated a form of betrayal that would be difficult for anyone to forgive, let alone trust the man. But Barnabas's generous spirit extended to his belief in Paul and consequently won over the other disciples to receive Paul, who we now know became a great man of God.

In Acts 15:36–39, Barnabas again demonstrates this act of generosity in another relationship. Paul and Barnabas were at odds—not over ministry, but over an individual, a younger John Mark. Paul thought he was still a "mama's boy" for leaving them earlier on a ministry trip and going back home, so he didn't want to take Mark with them on the next missionary journey. But Barnabas defended Mark; he opposed Paul and risked the very relationship in which he had invested so much time. Why? He so believed in Mark that he was willing to take that risk. Barnabas had a tremendous ability to believe in someone even when the person's actions did not fully warrant his trust. Just like he did with Paul, Barnabas extended his arm of generosity and reached out to Mark and included him in his missionary journeys.

Because of Barnabas's spirit of generosity, we know so much more about these two men, Paul and Mark. They are honored, respected, and applauded in Christian history, and rightly so. Let's not forget it was the generosity—of faith, finances, and grace—of the one named "Encourager" that is behind the ministries of these two men, and surely countless others. By the way, it's recorded in Colossians 4:10 and 2 Timothy 4:11 that Paul was thrilled to have Mark partnering in the ministry with him. Through Barnabas's generosity, a relationship is restored and the Kingdom is advanced.

We cannot do great things on this earth,
only small things with great love.
—*Mother Teresa*

MODELING GENEROSITY FOR OUR CHILDREN

What are ways to develop generosity in ourselves and our children? We can learn from Paul's illustration of the sowing of the seed.

Sow the Seed

First, God's principle is that if we sow cheap, we reap cheap; if we sow big, we reap big. Paul wrote, "Remember this: Whoever sows sparingly will also reap sparingly, and whoever sows generously will also reap generously" (2 Cor. 9:6). If you give a lot, you will get a lot back. So often our tendency is to hoard our time, talents, and possessions. Remember as kids how we gathered our toys around us and established them as ours and ours alone? We would form this protective barrier around our stuff and others could only play with them if we gave our permission—and often permission was given only upon parental intervention. We never had this problem with our third child. In fact, she never has money because she's always giving it away. Gabby is such a generous soul that we have to help her budget better, without killing her spirit of generosity.

But most of us are still pulling the toy-hoarding act. We hide our money away and only allot for others as is deemed charitably necessary or tax deductible. We protect our stuff with alarms and safes and establish our boundaries with fences. We're not saying we should all move into a commune and share everything. But have we come to a place in our hearts where our stuff is our stuff and nobody can touch it? Are we holding on to those things just a little too tightly? Is our value found in the quantity and quality of stuff we have, or in how much we can share and give away to others? God's principle says, "Give it away, and I will give you more to give away." What a great way to live: I have plenty, and you have plenty.

We recently learned that our son, Shay, had decided to give more than a 10 percent tithe. It was such a blessing to discover this. One day in a discussion about budgeting, he told us what he was doing. We were pleasantly shocked. His revelation led to an entirely different conversation about generosity and the excitement we felt about his decision. What a wonderful gift. Now, it doesn't make him any more spiritual than anyone else, and he doesn't know how long he will do this. But this experience has taught him that money is not just about him and getting more. Shay is learning that God blesses us to bless others by being generous.

Recognize the Owner

The idea of giving away is not so that we can get more, but is rooted in the fact that none of it is ours anyway. Look at 2 Corinthians 9:10:

"Now he who supplies . . ." What you hold on to is not yours; you're simply the manager. Everything we have—money, property, talents, time—is only because of generous gifts from our Father. And as believers, we must recognize the source of our "wealth." In living with Christ as Lord of our lives, we surrender all to Him, including our possessions, time, and talents. We recognize that they're not ours to keep but just to use for a short time in this world. So why would we hang on to them so tightly? We didn't deserve any of it and we won't leave this world with it. It doesn't bring us happiness, but it *can* be used to glorify the Father.

Rick Warren, in his book *The Purpose Driven Life*, tells the story of a couple offering Rick and his wife the use of their beachfront home in Hawaii for vacation.

It was an experience we could never have afforded, and we enjoyed it immensely. We were told, "Use it just like it's yours," so we did! We swam in the pool, ate the food in the refrigerator, used the bath towels and dishes, and even jumped on the beds in fun! But we knew all along it wasn't really ours, so we took special care of everything. We enjoyed the benefits of using the home without owning it.[1]

This is the way we should live every day. God owns everything on the earth. The Bible says, "The earth is the LORD's, and everything in it, the world, and all who live in it" (Ps. 24:1). Let's hold loosely those "things" we so value. Manage them well; love them not.

Live Purposefully

Living generously is really not that hard to do; we just need to live purposefully. Here are some opportunities to watch for:

1. *Give beyond yourself.* Begin to think of others first, rather than yourself. It's tough and will take work to develop this discipline. The Enemy wants us to focus on self because it's in our selfishness that we sin. Fight it. Work to consciously put all your thoughts through a "selfish filter." Ask yourself, "Am I thinking only of myself, or am I considering others and their feelings, needs, and desires?" Ask the Holy Spirit to guide your thinking in this way. As you do, you will see more and more people around you who need more of you. Doors will open to serve them as never before. Yes, we must first take care of our family, but there are so many others who can benefit from our labors. We have only one life. Use it generously giving to others as God has given to you.

Gabby is such a generous person that whenever she gets any money she finds ways to spend it *on somebody else.* She is a gift giver. So often, when she needed dollars, she wouldn't have any, because she had blessed someone else. *Do not discourage* this generosity in any way. Understand your children and help them to use their dollars wisely—either in being more generous or in budgeting appropriately to give it away.

2. *Find someone in need and minister.* There are 1,001 small but tangible ways you can bless someone every day. Seek them out and do for others. Even taking a moment to open a door for a stranger or call a sick friend is giving of yourself. People pass dozens of strangers every day without ever really seeing them. If we open our eyes to really see whom we are working beside, shopping with, or walking alongside, we may see opportunities to minister for God.

Look in unconventional places, too. Watch what people say on Internet social networks. One of your "friends" may have a need you didn't know about until you read it there. Now you can be a part of their solution and serve them with a heart of generosity.

3. *Find a place to serve.* Besides moments of spontaneous service, offer your services to a ministry or organization that focuses on helping others. Go to a homeless shelter or soup kitchen and donate your time to serve people who are less fortunate than you. Take a short-term mission trip or serve abroad. Check with your pastor for organizations that direct these kinds of ministries. Or maybe you just need to start in your own church by working with the children, playing an instrument in the band, or serving as an usher. You have more time than you realize. Analyze where you spend it: How much time is spent on you and how much time is spent on others? Are the scales tipped a little in the wrong direction? Lean the other way and give yourself to others.

LEGACY TRIP IDEA #14
Go to another country to participate in a mission project. Be sure to include a couple of days for sightseeing!

4. *Develop a giveaway fund.* Begin first with giving your 10 percent to the Lord. Then set aside what you will share with others. It doesn't have to be a lot. Start small. You'll be surprised at how much you can save and then use it to bless another person. Remember, it's not yours to begin with, so let someone else's needs be met. We can't give too much to God or to others.

Pastor Perry Noble told a story on his blog about a young man in his church. One day his assistant showed him a letter that had been sent to the church. A teenage boy wrote to Pastor Noble and said that he had been saving all his money for three to four years. He had held on to Christmas money, birthday money, and his earnings from his job. God had laid on his heart to give all this money to the church. The young man said, "Though it may seem a meager amount to the world, it is all that I have. I give this gift freely and with a light heart; after all, this money isn't really 'mine' to begin with. God can and will provide for me far better than I ever could. And it is an honor to know this money may help even just one person take a single step closer to God. That is a gift worth any price." In the envelope was a check for one thousand dollars.

We talk to our children a lot—I mean a *lot*—about being generous with more than just our resources. One phrase I (Jerolyn) often told our children when dropping them off for school was, "Smile today; someone might just need one." You see, just by being generous with our smiles and kindness we can benefit others. Generosity comes in a variety of shapes and sizes. It's not all about dollars. That's only one part of being generous. Generosity needs to become a way of life and a core value. Money then becomes just one way in which we can live generously.

TEACHING OUR CHILDREN GENEROSITY

It's very simple to teach children to be generous. They will learn best from watching you living a life of generosity. Remember, more is caught than taught. Then it's just a matter of watching for opportunities to encourage their generosity. They happen all the time. Look at how the principles from above can translate to our children's lives.

Give Beyond Yourself

Children are naturally selfish, so it's our job to guide them into a worldview that moves them outside of their selfishness. When they demand lunch to be made right now because they're hungry, don't immediately jump up. Finish what you're doing and then feed them. They are not going to starve. One step away from selfishness is learning that there is not always instant gratification. At the playground, when you see them pushing to the front of the line, hold them back to let others go first. They're going to have just as much fun and have the joy of allowing someone else to have fun, too.

Find Someone in Need and Minister

Look for those 1,001 ways. Here are some examples:

- You're in the park and a woman sitting on the bench drops her book. Ask your child to go and pick it up for her.
- A crying child's nose is running. Ask your child to get them a tissue.
- Someone drops a pen. Ask your child to get it and return it to the person.
- You send your child out to pull the trash cans back in from the curb. Have him or her bring up your neighbor's cans as well.

There are so many simple and easy ways to encourage generosity in our children. Opportunities are around us every day. As you encourage them to act on these opportunities, they'll develop the eyes to see for themselves. Then, whenever you see your children being generous, thank them for their generosity. Kids naturally want to please their parents. As they see this behavior pleasing you, they'll develop it further on their own.

Find a Place to Serve

This is definitely a mentoring opportunity. Whether you bring your kids with you to help when you're setting up chairs for an event at church or take them to work at a soup kitchen, you're serving alongside your children and working with them in giving your time away to others. Last summer, we had the privilege of taking our children to Mexico to build a house for a family of seven that was living in a small trailer in the poorest village we had ever seen. It was an amazing experience to be schlepping concrete, nailing down chicken wire, and laying roofing with our three teenagers. They sawed boards and spread tar with tenacity, even when some of the other workers were taking breaks in the shade. We were so proud of their untiring labor and generosity. While their friends back home were sleeping in till noon and hanging out at the pool, our kids were braving one-hundred-degree temperatures and twelve-hour workdays. They were truly serving with generosity.

I (Jim) was able to help out the local high school softball coach in digging holes for the softball fence. This was a great opportunity to do more than just work on a task, but also to build a relationship. So much of life is better when living it with others. We are designed to "belong" and not do life by ourselves. Investing your time in others is one of the greatest acts of generosity.

Develop a Giveaway Fund

This is an easy principle to teach to your children. Buy them each three jars—one for tithe (10 percent), one for savings (50 percent), and one for spending (40 percent). Every time money comes in, they should divide it up by percentage among the three jars. This develops the habit of tithing immediately and builds budgeting skills. Then encourage them to actively watch for where they can give from their savings or spending money to help someone else. Generosity begins with thankfulness for what we already have. No matter how little we own, there's someone in the world who has less. If we teach our children to live with thankful hearts and open eyes, generously giving of their finances and time will become a natural outpouring of thanksgiving.

PRACTICAL IDEAS FOR TEACHING GENEROSITY

Ages 2–5

- Establish play dates with other children. This way you can help your child learn the joy of sharing toys with friends.
- Do not immediately answer to your child's every whim. Children need to learn that they are not the center of everyone's world. Others must be considered.
- Read themed books on "helping others" to your children. Then demonstrate a helpful attitude at the playground or the store. Talk to them later about why you were generous in helping others.
- Establish an "others first" policy for things like getting in line, playing with a toy, and telling a story.

Ages 6–10

- Take your children with you when you volunteer or serve others. Let them help as much as they can.
- Train your children in gifts and tithes.
- Establish money jars—tithes (10 percent), savings (50 percent), and spending (40 percent). Encourage your children to keep their eyes open for ways to bless others with their spending money.
- At birthdays and Christmas or when donation bags come in the mail, have your child go through their belongings and pick out two or three nice things to give away.

Ages 11–17

- Take your children with you on mission trips.
- Teach the principle of "rounding up." If they owe someone money, instead of paying back the exact amount to the penny, round up. If they are asked to give two hours of their time to a task, instead they might give two and a half.
- Help your child find a place to volunteer their time helping others and utilizing their talents for another's benefit.

Parents

- Fight selfishness. Demonstrate generosity with your money, time, and possessions—within your family and with others.
- Always give more than is asked of you. Your children will see this trait in you.

QUESTION AND GIFT

Our gift for the core value of generosity is a dollar bill or a silver dollar. Although generosity isn't just about money (it also includes time and talents), the money is a good symbol of the things we can give away. Our question we often ask the kids is: "How are you doing with what you hold?" Are you clutching it tightly or sharing with others? Are you spending time to help others or to seek your own pleasures? Live a life of managing your resources—money, talents, possessions, and time—with an open-hand policy of generosity. It will come back to you tenfold.

Lord, make me a generous person—in word, grace, and time, with my money and possessions. Help me to see that everything I have and everything I am belongs to You and is not mine to own. You have blessed me so I can bless others. Help me to train my child to live with a generous spirit and to praise You with a heart full of generosity. Amen.

eight

SIGNIFICANCE

Gift: Framed picture of special people
Question: What difference are you making?

The alarm went off for the third time. Scott hit the snooze button one more time before dragging himself out of bed and into the shower. As the water beat down on his head, he couldn't help but sag with dread as he thought of his upcoming day. How was he going to push through one more day in such a dead-end job? His boss was constantly riding him about insignificant things because power had gone to his head and made him into a tyrant. Was it worth all this? "Yes, I'm paying the bills," Scott mused. "But at what price? There just has to be more to life than this."

UNDERSTANDING SIGNIFICANCE

When I'm dead and gone, what will I leave behind? What meaning does my life have? Am I really making a difference in the time I have?

What is my purpose for even existing? It seems as we get older, we ask these questions of ourselves more and more. They can haunt us with regret of a life lived in emptiness, or they can drive us to newer heights and challenges. The truth lies not in our success, but in our relationships—how we formed them and what we did with them. In this final core value we'll explore living a life of significance through loving, laughing, and learning. It's all about relationships.

THE SIGNIFICANCE OF JESUS

Jesus exemplifies all the core values, but we have chosen Him as the focus for this last value. By all societal standards of success, Jesus was a failure. He never got anywhere in His trade as a carpenter. One of His closest friends betrayed Him. And even though innocent of any crime, He was crucified on a cross at age thirty-three. But Jesus' life is not measured by His apparent human successes, but by His eternal significance. He left a mark on the lives of those He touched then and now.

Time has no meaning in itself unless we choose
to give it significance.

—Leo F. Buscaglia

As the ultimate example of living a life of significance, Jesus loved and lived as no other human being ever has. His example of walking with His fellow man while submitting to His Father provides a clear guide for how we're to live. Even those who don't believe in the divinity of Christ recognize and desire to emulate His ability to live as a superior human being.

Jesus, first and foremost, knew how to love. When asked which was the greatest commandment in the law, He said, "'Love the Lord your God with all your heart and with all your soul and with all your mind.' This is the first and greatest commandment. And the second is like it: 'Love your neighbor as yourself'" (Matt. 22:37–39). After giving the first command of surrendering our complete love to God, who is above all, Jesus commanded us to love each other, and then He demonstrated it with His life. Although He still took time away to be alone with His Father, His focus was on giving himself to others. He spent massive amounts of time teaching and living with others. Even when He was tired and wanted to draw away to be alone, He was there if the people called to Him:

> The apostles gathered around Jesus and reported to him all they had done and taught. Then, because so many people were coming and going that they did not even have a chance to eat, he said to them, "Come with me by yourselves to a quiet place and get some rest."
>
> So they went away by themselves in a boat to a solitary place. But many who saw them leaving recognized them and ran on foot from all the towns and got there ahead of them. When Jesus landed and saw a large crowd, he had compassion on them, because they were like sheep without a shepherd. So he began teaching them many things. (Mark 6:30–34)

Even in the midst of fatigue, Jesus' compassion and love for people prevailed. What an example! Jesus isn't teaching us to never take times of rest, but He's showing us a level of selflessness and compassion that we should all strive for. Jesus demonstrated a gracious life, and Paul exhorts us to do the same. He wrote,

If you have any encouragement from being united with Christ, if any comfort from his love, if any fellowship with the Spirit, if any tenderness and compassion, then make my joy complete by being like-minded, having the same love, being one in spirit and purpose. Do nothing out of selfish ambition or vain conceit, but in humility consider others better than yourselves. Each of you should look not only to your own interests, but also to the interests of others. Your attitude should be the same as that of Christ Jesus. (Phil. 2:1–5)

Jesus loved others well and without reserve. We can learn so much from Christ's practical examples of loving people. John 13:4–5 says, "So he got up from the meal, took off his outer clothing, and wrapped a towel around his waist. After that, he poured water into a basin and began to wash his disciples' feet, drying them with the towel that was wrapped around him." Culturally, this was a huge example of humility and service. Verse 12 says, "When he had finished washing their feet, he put on his clothes and returned to his place. 'Do you understand what I have done for you?' he asked them."

Do we understand? As if He hadn't humbled himself enough by coming to earth as a man, God incarnate lowered himself even further as a servant. We often spend too much time looking for God to give us the big assignments. Maybe we just need to take the time to learn how to use a towel. In *My Utmost for His Highest*, Oswald Chambers wrote, "We are not meant to be illuminated versions, but the common stuff of ordinary life exhibiting the marvel of the grace of God."[1] Live the ordinary in an extraordinary way.

Jesus had a tremendous capacity to love, but He never stopped growing and learning. Luke 2:52 says, "And Jesus grew in wisdom and stature, and in favor with God and men." Solomon also spoke to intellectual growth in Proverbs 9:9–12, saying,

Instruct a wise man and he will be wiser still; teach a righteous man and he will add to his learning. The fear of the LORD is the beginning of wisdom, and knowledge of the Holy One is under-standing. For through me your days will be many, and years will be added to your life. If you are wise, your wisdom will reward you; if you are a mocker, you alone will suffer.

To live a life of significance, we must first be gracious, and second, we must be growing. When we are through growing, we're through. Life becomes stagnant if we stay right where we are and never work to continue improving our minds and our hearts. Life without growth is like a seed lying forever buried in the soil. It has potential but never reaches its purpose for being. It can be the same with humankind. To reach our potential we must continue to learn, stretch, and grow our minds and our hearts—producing fruit through wisdom.

The most important function of education at any level is to develop the personality of the individual and the significance of his life to himself and to others.

—*Grayson Kirk*

The Bible doesn't give us any instances of Jesus breaking out in laughter, but it does talk about Him experiencing great joy: "At that time Jesus, full of joy through the Holy Spirit, said, 'I praise you, Father, Lord of heaven and earth, because you have hidden these things from the wise and learned, and revealed them to little children. Yes, Father, for this was your good pleasure'" (Luke 10:21). We can just imagine Jesus laughing it up with the Twelve out of His overwhelming joy at life, at the love of His Father, and at the relationships with His disciples. Laughter is good. Studies have even shown that laughter can cause our bodies to heal faster. Since all things good are made by God, feel the freedom to laugh with His joy and for His and our pleasure.

MODELING SIGNIFICANCE FOR OUR CHILDREN

Paul says we are to do *nothing* out of selfish ambition or vain conceit, but to always place others' needs first. A good principle to live by is JOY—Jesus, Others, You. When we do this, our priorities will fall into place. If we could accomplish this as a human race, imagine what life would be like. Hearts would be turned toward the Savior and His teachings. As a result, people would look out for the needs and desires of others first and deny self-promoting ambitions and comforts. It's not easy because it means consciously battling against our carnal nature. But it can be done. People are doing it every day.

A note of music gains significance from the silence on either side.

—*Anne Morrow*

Love

Recently our friends' four-year-old daughter was in the hospital with an undetermined bacterial virus. We received an e-mail from the child's mother thanking everyone for their prayers and "family" love during this difficult and stressful week. She told of one friend taking supper up to the hospital for her and her husband at ten o'clock at night. She said, "After having an IV put in your screaming four-year-old, there is something comforting about greasy Mexican food . . . But more importantly, you're family." It was foot washing in action—like Jesus would have done.

We can also do random acts of kindness every day for the people we come in contact with at the grocery store, gas station, or in our jobs. Moments where we step aside and let someone else go first. Times we take someone's empty cart back into the store for them. Even saying hello to a stranger as we pass in the parking lot can brighten the day of a fellow human being. There's so much pain and discouragement in our world that a smile and greeting may make all the difference in someone's life today. If we take time to look at other people—really look at them—we'll see a lot of pain and hurt that just needs some understanding and a kind word or gesture.

In *The Purpose Driven Life*, Rick Warren says "Love leaves a legacy." We can best demonstrate love with our time. He says, "The most desired gift of love is not diamonds or roses or chocolate. It is *focused attention.* Love concentrates so intently on another that you forget yourself at that moment."[2] What a beautiful way to state self-less love—focused attention. Take the time to look people in the eyes and concentrate on what they're saying when they're speaking, rather than just thinking about the next thing you want to say. We teach our children when they're little and learning to cross a street to "stop, look, and listen." This way they'll avoid being hit by a car. Maybe in our conversations we need to take the same caution—stop, look, and listen. In this way we avoid many dangerous obstacles of selfishness and are able to converse with another human being with compassion.

Learn

Part of our growth in significance is through reading. I (Jim) am not a reader, but I make it a discipline to read every day—mostly leadership books. Because my job involves so much leadership, I'm trying to grow in my knowledge of leadership and how to do it well. If you're a horse trainer, read up on horse training techniques. If you're a teacher, read up on teaching principles and learning styles. If you're a secretary, read up on customer service or time management. We're an information society, and we'll never lack for books and journals that will help us in an area we need growth. Take advantage of those opportunities.

Another way to grow is through hanging out with people who help you grow. Are you setting up those lunch or coffee appointments with people who speak wisdom into your life? Maybe you need to hang out with those who do the same job you do but have been doing it longer and have wisdom to pass along to you. Learn from those who have gone before you. You may avoid making the mistakes they had to live through.

Laugh

Third, live a life of laughter. Psalm 126:2 says, "Our mouths were filled with laughter." Ecclesiastes 3:4 tells us there is "a time to weep and a time to laugh." Nehemiah 8:10 says that "the joy of the LORD is your strength." Learn to live life grateful and goofy. Be happy, thankful, and looking for the joy in life. One of the best ways to get out of the gloom the Enemy can oppress us with is to consider what we're thankful for. Look for blessings—people and things for which to be thankful. Then express that joy of gratefulness to the Father and to each other.

Be thankful, but also laugh so hard that you hurt. Sometimes we become too serious and furrows begin to develop between our brows. We should take life and God seriously, but take ourselves less seriously. Laugh at your mistakes. Laugh at being silly. Laugh at the joy of living.

When our children were little, I (Jerolyn) always accused Jim of waiting until the kids' bedtime to have their good laugh for the day and thus get them all riled up and not ready to sleep. I love laughing with our teenagers during breakfast time. It starts the day off in such a positive light.

If a cluttered desk is the sign of a cluttered mind, what is the significance of a clean desk?

—Dr. Laurence J. Peter

John Ortberg tells a story in his book *The Life You've Always Wanted* about his daughter Mallory. He was giving a bath to his three children—one was in the bath, one in pajamas, and Mallory was standing there dripping wet and needing to be dried off. But instead of standing still for the ritual, she was doing her "Dee Dah Day" dance. This consisted of running in circles singing "dee dah day, dee dah day." It was just her special way of expressing the joy exploding in her heart. John writes,

On this particular occasion, I was irritated. "Mallory, hurry!" I prodded. So she did—she began running in circles faster and faster and chanting "dee dah day" more rapidly.

"No, Mallory, that's not what I mean! Stop with the dee dah day stuff, and get over here so I can dry you off. Hurry!"

Mallory stopped and simply asked her daddy, "Why?"

John had no answer. He had no place to go, no meetings to prep for, no sermons to write, nothing. He had just gotten into such a habit of hurrying from one task to another he almost missed the moment of joy his daughter was inviting him to experience.[3]

How many Dee Dah Day moments do we miss because we have an agenda and everyone and everything must fit neatly into it? How selfish can we be? We don't use the old phrase anymore "Stop and smell the roses," but maybe we should bring it back. Life continues chugging on and we have responsibilities, but we must take moments to just celebrate! So have a Dee Dah Day moment today. It will make you and everyone around you feel so much better.

What we do for ourselves dies with us. What we do for others and the world remains and is immortal.

—*Albert Pine*

TEACHING OUR CHILDREN SIGNIFICANCE

Children can be pretty self-centered. It's our job to help them learn to look outward to the needs of others and build healthy relationships. We can start at home and work our way out with many focused activities.

Teaching Children Love

Love and acts of love can come very naturally in a family if we purposefully look for ways to love. In our family, we all make sure we say "I love you" at least once every day. We never leave the house without saying "goodbye" and "love you." We've practiced this all our children's lives, so now it's a natural part of who they are.

We're also big huggers. A few years ago, our son started a routine with me (Jerolyn). He suddenly appears before me with his arms stretched out wide, and he doesn't move until I wrap my arms around his waist. He then enfolds me in a hug. These days, he's about 5'11", and I'm 5'3" so when I say enfolds, it's more like he swallows me up. And I love every minute of it. (If your teenager gives you a hug, never be the first one to release it. Wait for them to step back. You'll be amazed at how long they want to hold you in their arms.)

When Gabby was just a little thing—probably as soon as she could walk—she would run up to her daddy, raise her little arms as high as she could reach, and say, "Hold you, Daddy, hold you." She understood the power of loving with hugs.

Acts of love can be shown in ways other than physical affection. Encourage your children to do something nice for someone in the family. Even as little ones, they can pick up toys or go get a fresh diaper for a little brother or sister. Then show them how to take those acts of love outside the home. When taking a meal to a sick friend, let your little ones help you cook it and then take them with you to deliver it. Let them be a part of showing love to others. When going out shopping or to the park to play, talk about watching for ways to show kindness to others. Make loving a conscious lesson in your daily lives.

Learn

While you're demonstrating love, find ways to instill a love of learning in your children. From the time they're born, form a habit of reading to them every day. This can become a very special routine. Then as they get older, choose different kinds of books to grow them in different areas—science, history, biographies, literature, and mostly the Bible. Discuss with them what they've read so they see the usefulness and joy of reading.

Create moments of discussion with your children. Children are naturally curious. Instead of seeing their questions as annoying, discuss what they're interested in. You may even learn something in the process. Our evening family meal has always been our main time of discussion. But there are many moments in the car or when the kids come and flop by us on our bed that we just explore life with questions. Sometimes we have ready answers, sometimes we don't. But we always explore for the truth with our children.

As parents we're not the end all in our children's lives. There are so many wonderful people around them who can pour into their lives like we never could. Encourage healthy mentors in your children's lives. You are their first mentors, but they can learn valuable lessons from others as well. Just guide your children to the right influencers.

Laugh

Then there's laughter. Make it a point to laugh with each of your children at least once a day. Recently, Gabby, our fourteen-year-old, was hugging me (Jerolyn) and then tried to pull me over onto the couch. I resisted and held my footing. We had a wonderful time laughing at Gabby's attempts to pull me over and my near failure to stay on my feet. Too often, we parents feel such a weight of responsibility in our jobs, our community, and our families that we forget to live in joy and share that joy with our children. We have to take Dee Dah Day moments to just enjoy our kids and the life we have with them. We often sit with our kids and watch a good movie or comedian on DVD. Many conversations later are filled with quotes from those DVDs that make us laugh all over again. We created a shared experience that brings us joy again and again.

It's not hard to find ways to love, learn, and laugh; we just have to be purposeful about it. Keep your eyes open for the opportunities. Your lives will be enriched by the experiences.

PRACTICAL IDEAS FOR TEACHING *SIGNIFICANCE*

All Ages

- Instrut your child to do something for someone in the family without being asked, like making a sibling's bed.
- Encourage random acts of kindness. Before going out to run errands, tell your children to watch for others who need their help.
- Discuss together the "Why's" of life. Children are naturally curious. Instead of seeing their questions as annoying, discuss what they are interested in. You may even learn something in the process.
- Post funny notes around the house.
- With erasable markers, draw pictures on your children's bathroom mirror. When they stumble into the bathroom in the morning, they will smile.
- Watch a DVD of a wholesome comedy or stand up comedian. They provide wonderful, hilarious family entertainment so we can laugh together. Our kids extend the joy by repeating the jokes over and over.

Ages 2–5

- Look your child in the eyes when they talk to you and train them to do the same.
- Read voraciously to them. Take them to them to the library.
- Establish tickle time.

Ages 6–10

- Train your children to read for themselves.
- If your children have a hobby or sport, help them to learn more about it.
- Help your child to see needs in others and to figure out a way to help them.
- Be goofy with your kids. Have fun.
- Encourage your children to do their lessons not for grades, but to make them a better person.

Ages 11–17

- Provide lessons for your child for the hobbies or sports they enjoy.
- Encourage your child to hang out with other adults who will positively influence their life.
- Make family dinner a priority at least once a week. Talk, laugh, and cry together.
- Work with your child on the direction for their life. Encourage continued focus on future goals and aspirations.

continued

PRACTICAL IDEAS FOR TEACHING SIGNIFICANCE

- At this age, your kids will laugh *at* you more than *with* you. Laugh, too.
- Ask your kids about who they are influencing and how.
- Hug your teenager and never be the first one to release the hug.

Parents

- Love on your child every day at every age and say, "I love you."
- Laugh with them at least once a day.
- Help them learn in all areas of life—formally and informally.

SUMMARY

Significance—what will I be a part of that's bigger than me? Whose life will be positively impacted because of something I did? There's a huge difference between success and significance. We want our kids to have significance whether anyone ever says they were successful. It would be such a shame if people only saw us as a success and never as significant. But know this: If you and I are significant in our lifetime, then we will have been successful.

Living a life of significance can make a huge difference in the people around you and in your world. On April 21, 1855, a Boston Sunday school teacher by the name of Edward Kimball walked into a shoe store looking for one of his young class members, a clerk in the store. His intent was to lead the boy to the Lord. That young man received Christ right there in the storeroom; his name was Dwight L. Moody. Moody went on to be a preacher, and his passion for reaching the lost touched another minister in the British Isles, F. B. Meyer.

Meyer came to America and was speaking at a school where another minister heard him. Dr. Meyer challenged the crowd with, "If you are not willing to give up everything for Christ, are you willing to be made willing?" Those words changed the life of a young minister by the name of J. Wilbur Chapman. He began to preach at revival crusades, but after sensing a call back to the pastorate, he turned his ministry over to his crusade front man, Billy Sunday. Sunday went on to reach thousands with the gospel. In 1924, after Sunday spoke at a revival in Charlotte, North Carolina, a group of laymen formed an organization for continuing personal witnessing for Christ. In 1932, they planned another crusade in Charlotte and prayed for revival to come over that city, spread to the state, and then out to the ends of the world. As a result, Mordecai Ham began a meeting in 1934, in Charlotte, where a tall, lanky sixteen-year-old boy received Christ as his Savior. His name was Billy Graham. Dr. Graham went on to reach millions around the world for Christ. What an amazing journey from a Boston Sunday school teacher, to one of the greatest evangelists to ever live. But the story doesn't end there.

I (Jim) often say, "It's all about relationships!" Lately we have talked about finding some of those deeper friendships. We love, and we all long for, some of those lifelong relationships where we can be ourselves and share so much life together. We have been working hard at having "guest nights" where we entertain others and build those relationships.

On a Saturday in 1996, a young mother took her four-year-old son to the children's revival of the Billy Graham Crusade in their town. They sat clear up in the nosebleed section of the arena, but when it came time for the altar call, the mother leaned over to her son and said, "If you want to go down to receive Christ, I will walk down there with you." He shook his head and continued to sit and watch intently. After a few minutes, he tugged on his mother's sleeve and said, "I want to go down to the railing of the balcony." The two moved hand-in-hand to the railing. The mother knelt down and asked her son if he wanted to receive Jesus as his Savior, and he said yes. That little boy was Shay Bogear, our son. From Edward Kimball, to D. L. Moody, to F. B. Meyer, to J. Wilbur Chapman, to Billy Sunday, to Mordecai Ham, to Billy Graham, to Shay Bogear, who will be a college freshman this fall and is studying for the ministry. The torch of evangelism continues to be passed.

Do nothing out of selfish ambition or vain conceit, but in humility consider others better than yourselves. Each of you should look not only to your own interests, but also to the interests of others.

—*Philippians 2:3–4*

Edward Kimball chose to live a life that would touch others. Are you living a life of significance? Whose life are you touching for Christ? Who will they then touch for Christ, and so on and so on? You can make a difference. Live a life not for success, but for significance. Whether in a career in ministry or not, we are all ministers who can make a difference in the lives of those around us.

QUESTION AND GIFT

The key question for this core value is "What difference are you making?" And the gift is a framed picture of special people in your children's lives. The question is always in front of them: "How am I contributing to the lives of those I have influence on?"

It's pretty basic: Love God and love others. It's what we want our kids to be about. Live your life with love, learning, and laughter to help make a significant difference in the lives of others around you.

Lord, I want to be the complete person You would have me to be. I don't want to waste the little time I have been given here on this earth. Teach me to love with abandon, grow with passion, and laugh with joy. May I lead my child to live a life, not of selfish indulgence, but of significance for Your kingdom and glory. Amen.

FINAL THOUGHTS

Even though this book focuses on planning and preparing for a Legacy Trip, your work really begins when your children are young. Work hard to instill values in your children that will carry them throughout their lives. It can be difficult, but the rewards are great.

When planning the Legacy Trip, however, you also need to start early. Maybe set up a fund to save for the trip when your child is a baby. Putting away a little at a time will add up quickly.

Timeline

When your child is about eleven or twelve years old, start talking about the trip. Ask where he or she wants to go and what he or she wants to do. Dream and celebrate the process.

By the time the child turns thirteen, you should have decided on a location for your trip. Now it's time to make the plans final over the next few months—request vacation time, buy plane tickets if needed, make hotel reservations, etc. Don't put off these preparations. Make them a priority. Your child will only be fourteen once; don't miss it.

When you're on the trip, certainly take time to discuss the core values, but also just enjoy the person your child is becoming. God made him or her a unique individual that you have the privilege of helping to mold into an adult. Rejoice in that. Your child will never forget this time with you. It will be a memory that will last a lifetime and will remain a precious time when you showed your child just how much you love and care for his or her life.

When you come home from the trip, don't let it end there. Frame the core values and display them in your home. Talk about them periodically. Ask the questions. Reminisce about the trip.

The Legacy Trip obviously doesn't end our responsibility for our children. A couple of years ago, our oldest began college. We live in California, and she's attending school in Indiana. When we said our goodbyes and handed her off as a college freshman, I (Jim) took her beautiful face in my hands (with the rest of our family standing around) and told her how proud we are of her. I told her, with tears running down my face, that this is the reason we had raised her—to have her become her own adult who loves God and is an incredible person. I challenged her to begin to make her own legacy that she would leave for others—not only for her own children someday—but for all the others she will influence. And I challenged her to reach her incredible God-given potential. This can happen as a part of the Legacy Trip, but we chose to make it a separate "passing of the baton" to celebrate all God had designed in and for our child.

Keep these values alive in your home, and a legacy will continue with your children and your children's children.

appendix a

THOUGHTS FROM LAUREN ON HER LEGACY TRIP

I went to New York City for my Legacy Trip. I really enjoy theater and the arts, so naturally I was ecstatic to see Broadway musicals and experience the sights of New York City. That is just what we did—we saw three musicals while we were there. We ate hotdogs in Central Park, went shopping at the twelve-story Macy's, and took a bus tour through the city. My fondest memory about the trip was when my dad and I got all dressed up and took a cab to dinner and to see the musical *Thoroughly Modern Millie*. I had an amazing time, but exploring New York City was not all my dad and I did. We also talked about the core values my parents want us kids to take with us when we grow up and move out. They have been instilling these values in us since we were born, but they wanted to illustrate and lay them out for us before we go into high school and the rest of our lives.

Talk

I am the first child, so I got to be the guinea pig. Even though it was sometimes awkward talking about these things, because I had no idea what to say, I wish my dad and I had talked a little more about them. It's really important that you have a dialogue with your kids. Don't just talk about it and be done. Make sure they understand; force them (in a loving way) to talk with you about what they think of each core value. Fourteen-year-olds (teenagers in general) aren't big talkers when their parents ask what they think, so ask them specific questions that require more of an answer than "yeah," "no," "sure," or "whatever." (Mom and Dad have provided some sample questions in the Trip Notes in appendix C.) I'm not saying my dad and I didn't talk, or I didn't get anything out of the trip; I really did. I'm just saying I do wish I had been more talkative and discussed things more with him.

Others

Something I really liked was that after a few days in New York City, my dad and I headed to Connecticut to see some friends of ours. Since our topic that day was purity, Dad had them talk to me about their choices. This couple had stayed sexually pure until marriage, and they were able to share what they thought of the whole situation with me. I liked listening to what my dad thought and what he had to say about the different core values, but it was nice to get someone else's perspective. So, as someone who has been on the teenager end of this Legacy Trip, something I think you as parents should incorporate is to have other close, trusted friends or family put their two cents in just to mix things up a bit. This can be done by visiting them, having them write a letter to your child to be read on the trip, or even sending an e-mail or calling.

To the Teens

Now, to the teenagers—some of you, like me, will be totally stoked about this, and others . . . well, not so much. For some, spending any amount of time with the parents isn't very cool, but trust me, it's not torture and you'll survive. I mean, you get to go do something totally awesome that *you* choose, and you get all the attention. No siblings to bug you, no having to do what your little brother or sister wants to do; it's all you, baby! If you're not too sure about this whole thing, just be open-minded. Your parents love you and want to teach you some really cool things for your life before you up and leave them. Be willing to talk to them and share how you feel or what you think. This is your time, and I promise, your parents want to hear from you; they want to know what you have to say. Even if it's not about the core values, talk to them about things that interest you; teach them a thing or two about something you like to do. Just give them a little peek into your bubble so they know what's going on in your life, what you think, and how you feel about things. Whether you're one who is excited about this trip or not, don't make it so it's like pulling teeth for your parents. Answer their questions with more than a "yeah" or "mm-hmm." I'm not saying you have to share every secret of your life, but if there's a topic you're okay talking about, then share it; don't make them pry it out of you with the jaws of life!

One-on-One Fun

I was blessed with a dad who is a kid at heart, so there was no problem in the "having a good time" department. But just a note to the parents: Make sure your kid *is* having a good time. This trip is definitely meant as a learning experience, but it's also a vacation! If your kids aren't having fun, they aren't going to care what you have to say to them about the core values. Also, if you have kids that are close in age or are twins, don't, I repeat, *don't* roll both or all of their trips into one. This is supposed to be a one-on-one time with your kid. Calling home and checking in with the fam is fine, but don't take more than one child on the trip; it becomes less special, and they may not get to do what they want to do because they're having to compromise with a sibling.

After the Trip

This trip is the time to really lay out the core values for your kids, but talking about them shouldn't end there. After the trip and until they move out, continue discussing the core values. Ask them the questions that go along with each core value (i.e., "How high will you fly?"). Ask them how they're doing in each of the different areas. Are they showing integrity at school? Do they trust God with their life, future, etc.? Do they feel they have significance and are important to you and to God? This is a big one for teenagers. Some teenagers, especially ones with low self-esteem or with little self-confidence, get lost among their peers. It's easy to get caught up in the problems, drama, and social aspect of high school. So make sure they feel loved, and let them know they're significant, that God loves them and has a wonderful plan for their life (Jer. 29:11). Another thing is to periodically ask them if they remember the different values and what gift, biblical character, and question goes along with the core value—just to keep it fresh in their mind. Since my trip, I've had a hard time remembering the core values, and an even harder time remembering what each question, verse, and biblical character go with each value. One thing that may help is to type up your core values, frame them, and hang the frame somewhere the whole family will see it. It may even be a good idea to move it every once in a while just so it doesn't become another decoration, but something your family notices and pays attention to. Also, start talking to your kids about your core values before your trip. Even though you've been working to teach them these values their whole life, use the actual words, such as *significance* and *integrity*, when teaching your kids your values. In doing this, it'll help them better remember each value.

My Teens

The Legacy Trip is definitely something I want to do with my future kids. I think it's a great experience, and it's something they'll remember for the rest of their lives. When I do it, I may not have the exact same core values, and we may go about it in a different way and add our own special touches, such as maybe having both my husband and I go on the trip. Regardless of what we do, I want our Legacy Trip to be special and memorable specifically for our kids.

—Lauren Bogear Snider

PACKING YOUR HEART:
Pre-Trip Devotions for Parents

During the week or two before you venture out on this wonderful trip with your child, work through these devotions—one per day. They will prepare your heart and attitude for this amazing time. Our prayer is that this week solidifies in your heart the values you want to live, as well as getting you ready to share them with your precious child.

--- *day one* ---

DEVOTION

CHOOSE YOUR RESPONSE
Read Matthew 26:1–16.

- . . .will be handed over to be crucified. (v. 2)

- . . . an alabaster jar of very expensive perfume, which she poured on his head. (v. 7)

- Judas watched for an opportunity to hand him over. (v. 16)

These three scenarios sum up the three possible responses to Jesus—get rid of Him, love Him, or betray Him.

In verses 1–5, the chief priests and elders are plotting to have Jesus killed. They want to be rid of Him because He has upset their way of life. In the same way, the world wants to be rid of Jesus. He tends to rock the boat even two thousand years after He walked this earth. Those in opposition simply want Him to be gone. "I don't *need* Jesus" is the thought of the day. "I'm strong on my own; He is just a crutch for the weak and a wall for the intolerant to hide behind." They kill not just the idea of a Messiah, but Christ himself.

Then Jesus goes to Bethany, where a woman anoints Him with oil. She represents the believer who will give all to serve Jesus. He is treasured and adored, at the cost of our self-interest. Jesus is lifted up, loved, and prioritized in our lives. We may face ridicule, but we continue to raise Him up as the true God, the one and only Savior. Our hopes and dreams are centered on Him and His will. Our lives are not our own, but surrendered to the One who gives freedom through service. No longer are we bound by sin, because we serve the King of Kings and the Lord of Lords. His name is the only name we lift up in praise for He, and He alone, is worthy. Even if no one around us believes, we will stand on this truth.

Finally, there's the betrayal. Judas sells Jesus out. He's looking out for number one and abandons the very One who gave him life. Judas had lived and ministered with Jesus for three years, yet he still couldn't see the better way. He had witnessed miracle after miracle and prophecies fulfilled. He called Him Lord and Master while sitting at His feet, learning from His teachings. But "self" won the day, and Jesus was betrayed. How many people call themselves Christian yet sell Jesus out each and every day. When decisions must be made that might place Christ above personal wants and ambitions, He usually ends up on a shelf only to be dusted off for Sunday services. A heart that is not completely surrendered to Jesus will find that a commitment to His ways collapses under the pressures of the enticement of sin and selfish desires.

Crucify, anoint, or betray. How do you respond to Jesus?

Lord, if there is any area in my life that is not completely devoted to You, please reveal it to me so I can surrender it to You. I want every part of my being to glorify You and You alone. Amen.

INTEGRITY

THE WARNING
Read Matthew 18:6–9.

- Woe to the world because of the things that cause people to sin! (v. 7)

The graphic nature of Jesus' words immediately conveys the gravity of these sins. Not that any sin is not grave, but the punishments and the recommendations to prevent such sins borders on the extreme. He definitely wanted us to know that this is something He won't tolerate.

So are we taking these warnings seriously? We believe, as a society, we have hung our children out to dry. We haven't upheld a moral or ethical standard for them to follow. As parents, we are constantly rowing upstream against public opinions that would pollute our children's thinking.

Living a holy life that is pleasing to God is not just out of love for Him and a desire to spend eternity with Him. We're also held responsible for the people we influence. If there is any sin in our lives that leads someone else to sin, we are condemned. We don't have to be in leadership to be an example. If we're living an honest, open Christian walk, people are going to take notice. And they'll eventually know if there is sin in our lives. If we lead them down that path with us, we will be held accountable. That's a heavy responsibility we all must take seriously, and why Jesus says to eradicate the opposing offender. He's not saying we should literally mutilate our bodies, but He's emphasizing the seriousness of capturing our weaknesses and killing their influence.

Losing the lusts of our desires is nothing compared to losing eternity with God. We're not to live merely to satisfy every whim and notion we selfishly possess. Luke 10:27 says to "'Love the Lord your God with all your heart and with all your soul and with all your strength and with all your mind'; and, 'Love your neighbor as yourself.'" Nowhere in that passage are we told to love ourselves first or even second. Our comforts and desires are a tertiary point. And if we're loving God with our entire being (heart, soul, mind, and strength), then our first inclination will be to see others as God sees them and extend His love to them. If these steps are all in line, we won't lead someone to sin but only to God.

O Father, help me to first focus on loving You and then, out of that love, to love others. I again today die to self and the lusts that pull me toward the destruction of sin. Guide my heart; keep me for You alone. Amen.

—— *day three* ——

PURITY

GUARDED
Read Matthew 5:27–30.

- It is better for you to lose one part of your body than for your whole body to go into hell. (v. 30)

This is a tough subject to address. If we see a bunch of people walking around without a hand or an eye, we'll know we caused more confusion than clarity. So we'll begin with a basic understanding that adultery is a sin. Period. The Jews of that time would have understood that law. But now Jesus is saying that even looking at another person lustfully is the same as committing adultery. We've all turned our head to admire the beauty of a person of the opposite sex. But lust is taking it a step further, encompassing yearning or a desire to possess. Jesus views this very seriously—to the point of telling you to rid yourself of the offending part of your body so you will remember to not do it again.

The area of lust can be problem for women, but it's ten times more difficult for men. So we can only imagine what our teenagers are experiencing. And in a society that dresses skimpily, flaunts sexuality, and rampantly exhibits pornography in movies, print, and the Internet, it is no wonder that men and women are succumbing to the temptations bombarding them. That's why when we lead marriage retreats, we talk about the eye-gate and the ear-gate. God calls us to a life of holiness. If we're going to live as Christ lived and respect and honor our marriages and one another, we will guard our eyes and our ears to the best of our ability and consciously pay attention to what we're allowing to enter our ears and our eyes to affect our heart and mind. We can't be playing with fire and not expect to get burned. This is not a game; it's not a fantasy. People get hurt and lives are changed forever.

Today, choose to give someone's daughter or son respect by guarding your mind when you look at another person. It's a matter of heaven and hell.

Lord, You know the temptations that bombard me from every angle every day. Holy Spirit, guard my eyes and my ears from the temptations that are prevalent. Keep my mind and my heart pure for Your honor and glory. Amen.

POSITIVE ATTITUDE

AMAZED PRAISERS
Read Matthew 15:29–31.

- The people were amazed when they saw the mute speaking, the crippled made well, the lame walking and the blind seeing. And they praised the God of Israel. (Matt. 15:31)

One prayer request from our church recently said, "Anger and frustration. Praise God for help with my finances." We're not here to criticize the way a person expresses a prayer request. But we're looking at a larger principle here. Now, there are many good things about this request. First, she is bringing her request to God. She recognizes her anger and frustration as not right and is seeking His help. Also, she is giving Him praise for helping with her finances and by doing so, acknowledging God's work in her life. Those things are all good. What was striking was how one followed the other. Obviously, the situation causing these emotions is a legitimate need. But this request begs the question that if we spent more time praising God for the things He does do and standing in amazement over the miracle of His work in our lives, would we have to deal with as much pain in other areas of our lives?

How many times have we thanked God for an answered prayer and then moved right on to the next item for help? And that's if we remembered to thank Him. If we focused more on the amazing things He's doing in and around us, we would have very little to say to Him about the frustrations and difficulties. By focusing on His activity of love, our difficulties seem to lessen because we know God has it all under control. He's not going to leave us dangling at the end of a rope. If He is faithful in one area, He'll take care of us in all areas; that is His very nature. Maybe it will not be dealt with in the way we necessarily would choose, but He knows the best way for us, for Him, and for the kingdom of God.

We need to stop being whiners, complainers, and so needy. We can instead choose to be "amazed praisers." It won't be an easy change. Feeling needy is in our very nature. But we can do it with time and discipline. Oh, we will still lift our requests to Him; He tells us to ask. But maybe we will not feel so desperate each time because our mind is already set on His faithfulness in the past. So today be an amazed praiser. And do it again tomorrow. And the next day and the next until it just becomes a part of our first response. We serve a faithful God, and we need to be faithful to Him in return.

Lord, change my attitude from negative to positive through praise to You. You are my God and have my life under control. I will not live in the dregs of defeat, but see the good You provide in my life. Thank You, Lord. Amen.

GENEROSITY

A HEART FOR SERVICE
Read Matthew 20:20–28.

- Just as the Son of Man did not come to be served, but to serve, and to give his life as a ransom for many. (v. 28)

Here's a big surprise to many people who confess Christianity: We're here to serve. We are not here to soak up knowledge like a sponge. Gaining knowledge is good, but we must put it to work. We're not here to make money. We're not here to gain more power. We're not here to sit on our backsides and complain. We're not here to let everyone else serve us.

Jesus demonstrated that we're all called to serve others. Now, what that looks like will be different for different people. God has placed us all in various places on this globe at various times in history to do various jobs for Him. He has uniquely gifted each of us and will use those gifts to meet the needs of others and glorify Him. But no matter where we are, our service opportunities will range from large acts, such as helping someone rebuild their home after a disaster, to the smallest acts of service, such as holding a door open for someone. God wants our eyes to be constantly on the lookout for someone needing us to serve them.

However, before our eyes can see, our hearts must be in an attitude of giving; and that begins with surrender—surrendering our agenda with submission to God's. This isn't easy to do. We must constantly work to do better at living in ministry preparedness. Life can be messy and cannot always be plugged in to a day planner. Can you imagine Jesus waking up and saying, "Okay, today I am going to heal three blind people, one lame, and two deaf"?

Jesus lived in the moment of need. Several times He was walking one place and was interrupted with someone calling Him over to heal them or taking Him to their home to heal their child. And because Jesus had such a high level of compassion and a heart to serve, He went.

Now, I know we still have to do the things we need to do to live and to pay bills. But it wouldn't hurt us to focus more on living in the moment and letting God interrupt our schedule to go serve someone who needs it.

Lord, increase my heart compassion for others and their needs. Help me to remain focused on Your redirection from my daily tasks and live my life generously. Don't let me miss the moment because it doesn't fit my schedule. Amen.

SIGNIFICANCE

LOVE, LAUGH, LEARN
Read Genesis 48:1—50:14.

- All these are the twelve tribes of Israel, and this is what their father said to them when he blessed them, giving each the blessing appropriate to him. (Gen. 49:28)

This passage reflects in an ancient Jewish form the legacy we leave to our children. Jacob looked at each of his sons, and what they had done and what they could do showed him the ways he could bless their future. Jacob blessed them with a continuation of the life they had already built. They had made choices, and Jacob noted those choices as the destiny of their life. He also established the location of their tribe and provided a glimpse into their future.

As parents, we must know our children. Their individual personalities will take them on very different paths. It's our job to recognize the talents and gifts God has given to each of our children and encourage them to use those gifts to God's honor and glory. I doubt my children will be leaders of nations like Jacob's sons. That was a blessing from God that had been passed down from Abraham. But each of our children can have a great impact on the world for the glory of God. They can be leaders of the Christian nation if God so chooses to bless them in that way.

Our children need our blessing, encouragement, guidance, and love to follow the path God has for them to live. That's our greatest job—to be an example and guide to our children as the Lord would have us to. We know God has a lot of other jobs of service He wants us to complete. But discipling those three children is our first job. And what a joy it is to bless our children with the love of our Father and the hope of a future with Him.

Lord, help me to live a life of significance—loving generously, laughing freely, and learning voraciously—so my children have a positive example to emulate. I want my legacy to live on in their lives. Amen.

TRIP NOTES
Core Value 1: Devotion

Biblical Character: Peter

Scripture: It is Jesus' name and the faith that comes through him that has given this complete healing to him, as you can all see. (Acts 3:16)

Living as a Christian teenager today can be a huge challenge. You want to follow God, but you have so many pressures and temptations around you every day. Friends are constantly pulling you one way, parents another, and your desires still another. Homework and chores are piling up. You want to have fun, but not be stupid about it. How do you know how to live in this world, make right choices, and still be a child of God?

Peter, one of Jesus' disciples, lived daily with the Master. He learned under the Almighty himself. Yet Peter did not immediately nor fully understand the power of God and the complete commitment to which Christ was calling him. In Matthew 14:22–31, when the disciples see Jesus walking on the water, Peter is the only one to ask Jesus to let him walk out to the Master. Peter gets out of the boat and walks on the water. But when the wind and waves increase, he takes his eyes off the

Master and looks at the waves crashing around him. That's when he begins to sink, demonstrating his lack of complete devotion to and trust in the power of Jesus.

But by the time Jesus was crucified, risen, and ascended to heaven, Peter had learned to walk a very different faith. In Acts 3:1–8, we learn of a man, crippled from birth, asking Peter and John for money. "Then Peter said [to the man], 'Silver or gold I do not have, but what I have I give you. In the name of Jesus Christ of Nazareth, walk.' Taking him by the right hand, he helped him up, and instantly the man's feet and ankles became strong" (vv. 6–7). Peter now had enough faith to help others walk in spite of the storms, because he had placed his complete trust in Jesus Christ. He finally understood the meaning of loving God with his entire being—heart, soul, mind, and strength.

STUDY QUESTIONS

1. How did Peter's attitude change from when he walked on the water to his healing and preaching in Acts?

(Peter had some faith, but wasn't living in abandon, because he took his eyes off Jesus. He hadn't learned to trust Jesus as his Lord.)

2. What had happened to change Peter's outlook between these two events?

(Jesus had been crucified and raised from the dead.)

3. How does the cross change our view of Christ?

(We see Him not just as an historical figure or a religious leader, but as the Son of God and Savior of humankind and can enter into a personal relationship with Him.)

4. What does it mean to surrender to Jesus to be Lord of your life? *(Surrendering to the Lord goes beyond accepting Him as forgiver of my sins. It's complete devotion—trusting in Him for everything, opening every door of my heart to His leading. It's not living for me anymore, but living only for His will and glory.)*

VALUE QUESTIONS

1. What ways can you love God with your heart? *(Study His Word, pray, and worship.)*

2. What ways can you love God with your soul? *(Surrender to His will for my life.)*

3. What ways can you love God with your mind? *(Follow His teachings without compromise.)*

4. How can you love God with more of your strength? *(Serve others.)*

The Gift: Skeleton key
The Question: Who holds your key? The key to your heart can be given away to many people or things. Only God should hold that key—total surrender.

TRIP NOTES
Core Value 2: Integrity

Biblical Character: David

Scripture: The LORD does not look at the things man looks at. Man looks at the outward appearance, but the LORD looks at the heart. (1 Sam. 16:7)

Integrity is a value that is challenged in the teen culture every day, whether a friend asks you to lie or cover up something, or you're tempted to do your work in the least possible time and effort. Loyalty is reserved for school ball teams, the closest friendships, and a few rare schoolteachers. The ideal of staying loyal to one spouse has been abandoned by many adults, with lasting marriages being more and more a rarity. Commitments to marriage, jobs, or school are made with the qualifier "if I feel like it" attached to them. So it's no wonder that it's tough today to be a person of integrity. Everything is fighting against you being the person you know you should be. But it is possible.

David was an exceptional young man. He is first introduced to us in 1 Samuel, where God tells Samuel to anoint him as future king of Israel. A simple shepherd boy, he had been chosen to lead God's people. David's reputation as a young man blessed by God grew, and soon King

Saul brought him into his house as a musician. One day David's father, Jesse, sent David with food and supplies to the battlefield where his older brothers were fighting in Saul's army against the Philistines. As David approached, he heard one of the Philistines, Goliath, calling out a challenge to the Israelites as he had done every day for forty days. Goliath was a huge man who stood over nine feet tall. Just the very sight of him put fear into most men, and no one had taken up the challenge to fight him.

But David was not afraid. He had been raised knowing that the Israelites were God's chosen people. He knew all the stories of how God had delivered the Israelites in the past in miraculous ways. David stood firm in the belief that God can do what He says He can do and that no Philistine could overcome God's chosen people. His loyalty to God and to the people of Israel pushed him forward to meet Goliath's challenge.

Armed with only five stones and a slingshot, young David walked forward to the battle lines to face off with the fully armored giant. With one well-placed stone, David brought down the mighty Goliath and won the victory for the Israelites.

STUDY QUESTIONS

1. What do we learn about David from this story?

(He worked hard for his father; man of his word; stood up for what he believed; loyal to Israel.)

2. Why do you think David was the only one who would face up to Goliath's challenge?

(He chose to honor God and himself by living his life true to his word, country, and responsibilities. He knew he served a big God and stood firm on what he believed.)

VALUE QUESTIONS

1. What is integrity?
(Maintaining high moral principles—living a life of truth.)

2. How hard is it to lose and then regain integrity?
(To get your integrity back, you have to build trust back with the people around you. If you lie, you have to tell the truth. If you don't meet a responsibility, you must work hard to always be where you said you will be.)

3. What do you face at school, at home, and at work that challenges your integrity?
(Temptations to lie; not wanting to do chores, but needing to follow through without being told; loyalty tested through working under difficult people.)

4. What do you need to do to protect your integrity?
(Choose to give God my very best in everything I do. Speak truth; work hard; be responsible; remain loyal to those in authority over me.)

The Gift: Mirror
The Question: How's the mirror looking? If you can look in the mirror and both you and God are pleased, then it doesn't matter what others think. In fact, if you are demonstrating true integrity, what others think will not be an issue.

TRIP NOTES
Core Value 3: Purity

Biblical Character: Joseph
Scripture: And though she spoke to Joseph day after day, he refused to go to bed with her or even be with her. (Gen. 38:10)

In today's society, teenagers and adults are bombarded with sexual images, lyrics, and language all the time. We can't turn on the TV, radio, or go to a movie without being confronted with temptations that entice our minds to think about sex. Many teens face pressure from friends or those they're dating to take the "next step" in their relationships. We seem to be facing an uphill battle when it comes to remaining sexually pure. But hear us: It's possible to save yourself until marriage. Others have done it, and with God's help, you can, too. Not only are you being obedient to God's laws, but you're saving something very special for the person you will be with for the rest of your life.

Joseph was an amazing young man of character. As we read about his life in Genesis 37–50, a picture emerges of a man who was devoted to God and truth even in the middle of terrible difficulties and unfair events in his life. Sold as a slave by his own brothers, Joseph found himself living and working in Egypt for a very powerful man. One day, his owner, Potiphar, was gone from the house and Joseph was left in charge. That's when Potiphar's wife decided to seduce this handsome young man. Joseph could have submitted to her requests, but instead he chose to honor his God and his master and literally ran from the temptation Potiphar's wife placed before him. He knew that a few moments of pleasure were not worth the consequences of disobedience to God's laws or dishonoring his master.

Sexual purity can seem very old-fashioned to a young, modern mind. But the principle God applied to Joseph's life still applies to our lives today. Joseph had the same desires and temptations we face. The difference is that Joseph consciously chose to honor God and remain pure. You can make that same choice.

STUDY QUESTIONS

1. Are sexual temptations normal?
(Absolutely. God designed us to experience and enjoy sex, but only in the context of marriage.)

2. Does the Bible really say you can't have sex before marriage or outside of marriage?
(Yes, God's design began with Adam and Eve—one man for one woman. But He also speaks against fornication in Scripture. See Genesis 2:25 and 1 Corinthians 6:9–20.)

VALUE QUESTIONS

1. What types of sexual temptations do you face?
(TV, movies, people wearing revealing clothing, Internet or printed pornography, enticing thoughts, pressures by friends/special someone.)

2. How can you protect yourself against giving in to sexual temptations?
(Guard the eye-gate and ear-gate. Be careful of the types of TV, movies, literature, and music I watch and listen to.)

3. If in a relationship, in what ways will you determine now to remain pure?
(Determine that this is a commitment to purity I will keep. Talk to my partner about my commitment. Decide to avoid situations where I would be tempted to have sex.)

The Gift: Ring
The Question: What's on your hand?

TRIP NOTES
Core Value 4: Positive Attitude

Biblical Character: Paul

Scripture: But we have this treasure in jars of clay to show that this all-surpassing power is from God and not from us. (2 Cor. 4:7)

No one is ever short on things to complain about. If you talk to pretty much anyone, somewhere in the conversation you'll hear a negative attitude about school, relationships, work, the weather, the economy; you name it. Negative attitudes surround us every day. Many people have some really serious problems, but if you really listened to how we talk, you'd think that *most* of us live in poverty, loneliness, and despair with few blessings to count. With so much negativity around us, it's no wonder we fall into that trap and fail to keep a positive attitude.

No matter what problems we have, very few of them can compare to the problems and suffering the apostle Paul faced. Paul started out as a persecutor of Christians. He hunted them down and put them in prison because he believed they were going against God and the Jewish traditions. But God got hold of his heart, and Paul made a 180-degree change. He became completely on fire for God. In fact, Paul generously shared that fire. Many of the books of the New Testament are letters Paul wrote to encourage the baby churches in the first century. But Paul's enthusiasm for God and sharing His love came with a price.

During Paul's ministry, he was beaten, imprisoned, shipwrecked, sick, hungry, and destitute. But through it all he maintained a positive attitude. In 2 Corinthians 4:7–9, he says, "But we have this treasure in jars of clay to show that this all-surpassing power is from God and not from us. We are hard pressed on every side, but not crushed; perplexed, but not in despair; persecuted, but not abandoned; struck down, but not destroyed." Paul knew that our bodies are temporary and that life is short. It didn't matter how he was treated; he had only one purpose—to share the gospel of Jesus Christ with the world. Because of his singular focus and his unwavering devotion to God, Paul chose to live with a positive attitude no matter what was done to him. His can-do attitude soared high above his temporary troubles.

STUDY QUESTIONS

1. Did Paul deserve the punishments and persecution he was suffering?

(No, he was simply living out his belief in Jesus Christ and sharing it with others.)

2. How did Paul maintain a positive attitude through so many difficulties?

(Paul put his trust in God alone. He kept his heart focused on the job he needed to do and knew that the suffering was only for a little while. Comfort here on earth was not Paul's goal; heaven was his hope.)

VALUE QUESTIONS

1. What events cause you to lean toward a negative attitude?
(Not getting my way; doing something poorly; listening to others being negative.)

2. How can you view those events in a more positive light?
(Look at the positive side of every situation. Choose to see the glass half full instead of half empty.)

3. What steps can you take to maintain a more positive attitude?
(Choose people to hang out with that are positive; have a regular time alone with the Lord—preferably every day; focus on others and their needs; choose a positive attitude in everything.)

The Gift: Eagle
The Question: How high will you fly?

TRIP NOTES
Core Value 5: Generosity

Biblical Character: Barnabas

Scripture: Joseph, a Levite from Cyprus, whom the apostles called Barnabas (which means Son of Encouragement), sold a field he owned and brought the money and put it at the apostles' feet. (Acts 4:36–37)

Generosity doesn't seem to be the primary thought for most people. Usually our first reaction is to take care of ourselves. We want to be sure we have enough money to live the way we want to live and do the things we want to do. We choose to do activities that are fun and entertaining for us. If we're uncomfortable, we work at making ourselves more comfortable by any means. Even when someone is in need, we will often decide whether or not we'll help them based on how convenient or inconvenient it is to us.

Barnabas lived by a completely different set of rules. His life was one of giving and giving generously. We know from reading the book of Acts (4:37) that Barnabas generously gave money to the apostles to help the spreading of the gospel of Jesus Christ. He once sold a field and handed all that money over to the apostles. He understood that the need to get the message out was more important than his need for that money.

While sharing our money and possessions with others who are in need is vital, we can be generous with so much more than our finances. Barnabas also demonstrated his generosity by believing in others. As we read in Acts 9, Saul (also known as Paul) was a man who had been persecuting the followers of Jesus and then was converted to Christianity in a very dramatic way. Three years later Paul went to Jerusalem to join the disciples' work there. But when he arrived, the disciples didn't want anything to do with Paul. They knew of the persecution he had caused and were afraid of him. But Barnabas saw Paul for who he really was, a person changed by the power of Jesus Christ. Barnabas took Paul to the disciples and explained his journey to them. Because of Barnabas's word of faith in Paul, the disciples accepted him into the ministry there. If it hadn't been for Barnabas and his generous belief in Paul, we may not have had the writings of one of the greatest teachers in the Bible. Barnabas looked outside of himself and took a stand for a man who was misunderstood and who could make a huge difference in the world.

We, like Barnabas, can demonstrate a generous spirit in many areas of our lives—finances, time, encouragement, support, grace. We have the capacity to give in service to others and in doing so, serve our Lord. Living generously will bring a joy to your life that you will never have without giving. The Lord says He blesses a cheerful giver. Give of yourself generously out of a heart of love for God and others. He will bless you for it.

STUDY QUESTIONS

1. How did Barnabas demonstrate generosity?
(Finances, belief in Paul, grace and encouragement.)

2. What was Barnabas's motivation to be a generous person?

(He loved God and understood the mission of telling others about Jesus Christ. His service and generosity did not come from a command or ritual, but from a love in his heart for his heavenly Father.)

VALUE QUESTIONS

1. Are you tithing? Are you giving above your tithe?

2. How are you giving of your time to God? What more could you do?

(Helping a neighbor or friend; serving at a shelter; bagging up used toys or clothes for those in need, etc.)

3. How are you using your talents for God? What more could you do?

(Serve somewhere at church in music, helping with the children, maintenance, etc.)

4. What attitude should we have in giving? Why?

(We should give out of a love for God and others because God has not only created us to be generous, but tells us to do it cheerfully.)

5. What other ways could you live generously?

(Extend grace to others; be quicker to forgive; smile more; not expect more from others than I do myself.)

The Gift: Dollar bill or silver dollar
The Question: How are you doing with what you hold?

TRIP NOTES
Core Value 6: Significance

Biblical Character: Jesus

Scripture: And Jesus grew in wisdom and stature, and in favor with God and men. (Luke 2:52)

A popular phrase a few years ago was "What Would Jesus Do?". A whole movement filled with T-shirts, bracelets, and hats came out of this one question. In living a life of significance, we're essentially asking the same question: "What would Jesus do?" We certainly couldn't pick a better person to emulate. If we study how Jesus chose to live and what relationships He formed, we will gain insight into how to live our lives to the fullest.

Jesus surrounded himself with three different groups of people—His family, His disciples, and the mass followers. Growing up, He learned the carpentry trade from His father. He had brothers and sisters and learned all the traditions and ideas of being a Jew and following God. He was always, even as a child, one who sought to better himself and those around Him. Luke 2:52 says Jesus "grew in wisdom and stature, and in favor with God and men."

Jesus' ministry began and ended with His mother and disciples nearby. They were a part of who He was on this earth, and He chose to live in close relationship with them. Even within the group of His disciples, Jesus chose Peter, James, and John as His inner circle—the ones He spent the most time with. They ate together, worked together, and traveled together. As they walked through life, Jesus poured himself into the Twelve through teaching about love, life, and giving of themselves. He scolded them when they were wrong one day. On another day, He got down on His knees and demonstrated true servanthood by washing their dirty feet. Jesus lived out a love they had never before known and changed their lives forever.

STUDY QUESTIONS

1. Who did Jesus have relationship with?

(His family, His friends, the disciples, the people who came to hear Him speak.)

2. How did Jesus show love?

(Healing, extending mercy, taking the time to meet with the people, making sure the people's needs were met, teaching the people about repentance, demonstrating how to live, dying on a cross—sacrifice.)

3. Who brought Jesus joy?

(His Father, the disciples, the people who followed Him, His family.)

4. How do we know Jesus believed in learning?

(He taught the people in the synagogues and on the mountainsides.)

VALUE QUESTIONS

1. Who do you have relationships with?
(Parents, siblings, friends, neighbors, coworkers, classmates/teachers, etc.)

2. How do you express your love to those around you?
(Thinking of their needs before my own; spending time enjoying life together.)

3. Do you spend time laughing every day? Why or why not?

4. In what ways do you need to continue growing in knowledge of life, God, yourself, and others?
(Reading the Word and other encouraging books; take myself less seriously; spend time enjoying family and friends; laugh.)

The Gift: Framed picture of special people
The Question: What difference are you making?

appendix d

TRAVEL LOG

Parent

DAY 1: DEVOTION

What did we do today? _____

_____

_____

_____

_____

_____

_____

What was my favorite part of the day? _____

_____

_____

_____

_____

_____

_____

_____

What do I want my child to learn about devotion? _____

_____

_____

_____

_____

_____

_____

_____

_____

_____

How will I help my child accomplish devotion? _____

_____

_____

_____

_____

_____

_____

_____

_____

_____

_____

TRAVEL LOG

Child

DAY 1: DEVOTION

What did we do today? _____

_____

_____

_____

_____

_____

_____

What was my favorite part of the day? _____

_____

_____

_____

_____

_____

_____

_____

What did I learn today about devotion?_____

_____

_____

_____

_____

_____

_____

_____

_____

How am I going to make devotion a part of my life? _____

_____

_____

_____

_____

_____

_____

_____

_____

TRAVEL LOG

Parent

DAY 2: INTEGRITY

What did we do today? _____

_____

_____

_____

_____

_____

_____

What was my favorite part of the day? _____

_____

_____

_____

_____

_____

_____

What do I want my child to learn about integrity? _____

_____

_____

_____

_____

_____

_____

_____

_____

_____

How will I help my child accomplish integrity? _____

_____

_____

_____

_____

_____

_____

_____

_____

_____

TRAVEL LOG

Child

DAY 2: INTEGRITY

What did we do today? _____

_____

_____

_____

_____

_____

_____

What was my favorite part of the day? _____

_____

_____

_____

_____

_____

_____

_____

What did I learn today about integrity? _____

_____

_____

_____

_____

_____

_____

_____

_____

_____

How am I going to make integrity a part of my life? _____

_____

_____

_____

_____

_____

_____

_____

_____

_____

TRAVEL LOG

Parent

DAY 3: PURITY

What did we do today? _____

_____

_____

_____

_____

_____

_____

What was my favorite part of the day? _____

_____

_____

_____

_____

_____

_____

_____

What do I want my child to learn about purity? _____

_____

_____

_____

_____

_____

_____

_____

_____

_____

How will I help my child maintain purity? _____

_____

_____

_____

_____

_____

_____

_____

_____

_____

_____

_____

TRAVEL LOG

Child

DAY 3: PURITY

What did we do today? _____

_____

_____

_____

_____

_____

_____

What was my favorite part of the day? _____

_____

_____

_____

_____

_____

_____

_____

What did I learn today about purity? _____

_____

_____

_____

_____

_____

_____

_____

_____

How am I going to make purity a part of my life? _____

_____

_____

_____

_____

_____

_____

_____

_____

_____

TRAVEL LOG

Parent

DAY 4: POSITIVE ATTITUDE

What did we do today? _____

_____

_____

_____

_____

_____

_____

What was my favorite part of the day? _____

_____

_____

_____

_____

_____

_____

_____

What do I want my child to learn about having a positive attitude?

_____

_____

_____

_____

_____

_____

_____

_____

_____

_____

How will I help my child maintain a positive attitude? _____

_____

_____

_____

_____

_____

_____

_____

_____

_____

_____

_____

TRAVEL LOG

Child

DAY 4: POSITIVE ATTITUDE

What did we do today? _____

_____

_____

_____

_____

_____

_____

What was my favorite part of the day? _____

_____

_____

_____

_____

_____

_____

_____

What did I learn today about having a positive attitude? _____

_____

_____

_____

_____

_____

_____

_____

_____

How am I going to make a positive attitude a part of my life? _____

_____

_____

_____

_____

_____

_____

_____

_____

_____

TRAVEL LOG

Parent

DAY 5: GENEROSITY

What did we do today? _____

_____

_____

_____

_____

_____

_____

What was my favorite part of the day? _____

_____

_____

_____

_____

_____

_____

What do I want my child to learn about generosity? _____

_____

_____

_____

_____

_____

_____

_____

_____

_____

How will I help my child live a life of generosity? _____

_____

_____

_____

_____

_____

_____

_____

_____

_____

TRAVEL LOG

Child

DAY 5: GENEROSITY

What did we do today? _____

_____

_____

_____

_____

_____

_____

What was my favorite part of the day? _____

_____

_____

_____

_____

_____

_____

What did I learn today about generosity? _____

_____

_____

_____

_____

_____

_____

_____

_____

How am I going to make generosity a part of my life? _____

_____

_____

_____

_____

_____

_____

_____

_____

_____

_____

TRAVEL LOG

Parent

DAY 6: SIGNIFICANCE

What did we do today? _____

_____

_____

_____

_____

_____

_____

What was my favorite part of the day? _____

_____

_____

_____

_____

_____

_____

_____

What do I want my child to learn about significance? _____

_____

_____

_____

_____

_____

_____

_____

_____

_____

How will I help my child accomplish significance? _____

_____

_____

_____

_____

_____

_____

_____

_____

_____

TRAVEL LOG

Child

DAY 6: SIGNIFICANCE

What did we do today? _____

_____

_____

_____

_____

_____

_____

What was my favorite part of the day? _____

_____

_____

_____

_____

_____

_____

_____

What did I learn today about significance? _____

_____

_____

_____

_____

_____

_____

_____

_____

_____

How am I going to live a life of significance?_____

_____

_____

_____

_____

_____

_____

_____

_____

_____

_____

NOTES

Preface
1. Laurence Steinberg, "7 Rules for Parents," *Time*, May 10, 2004, 65.

One: The Legacy Trip
1. *Merriam-Webster's Collegiate Dictionary*, 11th ed., s.v. "Rite."
2. http://www.thewildwest.org/native_american/religion/Quest.html.
3. "Quinceañera," http://en.wikipedia.org/wiki/Quincea%C3%B1era.
4. "Coming of age," http://en.wikipedia.org/wiki/Coming_of_age.
5. "Confirmation," http://en.wikipedia.org/wiki/Confirmation_%28sacrament%29.
6. "Bar Mitzvah," http://en.wikipedia.org/wiki/Bar_mitzvah.
7. Claudia Wallis, "What Makes Teens Tick," *Time*, Sept. 26, 2008, 3, http://www.time.com/time/magazine/article/0,9171,994126-3,00.html.
8. Ibid.

Two: The Legacy of Character
1. "Ronald Wilson Reagan, Commencement Address 1993," http://pao.citadel.edu/reagan.

Four: Integrity
1. John Maxwell, *The Maxwell Leadership Bible* (Nashville: Thomas Nelson, 2002), 389.
2. Stuart Briscoe, sermon, Founder's Week of Moody Bible Institute, Chicago, Ill., February 1986.
3. H. Jackson Brown Jr., *Life's Little Instruction Book* (Nashville: Rutledge Hill Press, 2000), as quoted in *Reader's Digest*, June 1996, 57.

4. "FaithWalk," in *The Toolkit*, Changing Church Forum, February 24–25, 2007, p. 13.

Five: Purity

1. Joe McIlhaney and Freda McKissic Bush, *Hooked: New Science on How Casual Sex is Affecting Our Children* (Chicago: Northfield, 2008). Quoted in Chuck Colson, "Hooked: Sex, Science, and Spirituality," *Breakpoint Commentary*, March 18, 2009, www.informz.net/pfm/archives/archive_784106.html.

Six: Positive Attitude

1. Francie Baltazar-Schwartz, "Attitude Is Everything," as quoted in Jack Canfield, *Chicken Soup for the Soul at Work* (Deerfield Beach, Fla.: Health Communications, 1996).

Seven: Generosity

1. Rick Warren, *The Purpose Driven Life* (Grand Rapids, Mich.: Zondervan, 2002), 45.

Eight: Significance

1. Oswald Chambers, *My Utmost for His Highest* (Westwood, N.J.: Barbour, 2006), 121–122.
2. Rick Warren, *The Purpose Driven Life* (Grand Rapids, Mich.: Zondervan, 2002), 125, 127.
3. John Ortberg, *The Life You've Always Wanted* (Grand Rapids, Mich.: Zondervan, 2002), 59–60.